Beerbohm's
Literary
Caricatures

The Poets' Corner [1904]

Courtesy of the William Andrews Clark Memorial Library, University of California, Los Angeles

HD 1420

The drawing shows Max Beerbohm shining a torch on a statue-bust in Poets' Corner, Westminster Abbey, London. It was used for the front cover of *The Poets' Corner* (1904), Max Beerbohm's second collection of caricatures

Beerbohm's Literary Caricatures

From Homer to Huxley

Selected,
introduced,
and annotated
by

J. G. RIEWALD

ARCHON BOOKS 1977

First published 1977 as an Archon Book
an imprint of The Shoe String Press Inc
Hamden Connecticut 06514

Printed in the United States of America

Library of Congress Cataloging in Publication Data

Beerbohm, Max, Sir, 1872-1956.
Beerbohm's literary caricatures.

Bibliography: p.
Includes index.
1. Authors—Caricatures and cartoons. 2. English wit and humor, Pictorial. I. Riewald, Jacobus Gerhardus. II. Title.
III. Title: Literary caricatures.
NC1479.B37R53 1977 741.5'942 77-3974
ISBN 0-208-01632-5

To Elisabeth

Contents

Acknowledgments

For general permission to reproduce those of Max Beerbohm's drawings that appear in this book and to quote passages from his writings I am indebted to Mrs. Eva G. Reichmann, Administratrix of the Estate of Sir Max Beerbohm, and her representative, Sir Rupert Hart-Davis.

Acknowledgments and thanks are due to the publishers of the albums from which a number of the Beerbohm drawings are reproduced: William Heinemann Ltd., London, for *The Poets' Corner, Fifty Caricatures, A Survey, Things New and Old,* and *Observations*; Dodd, Mead & Co., New York, for *The Poets' Corner*; and Methuen & Co. Ltd., London, for *A Book of Caricatures.*

Grateful acknowledgment is also made to the following libraries, galleries, museums, and institutions, whose authorities have generously given me permission to reproduce photographs of drawings in their possession: the Humanities Research Center, the University of Texas at Austin; the Birmingham Museums and Art Gallery, Birmingham; the Lilly Library, Indiana University, Bloomington, Indiana; Charterhouse School, Godalming, Surrey, England; the Department of Printing and Graphic Arts, Harvard College Library; the Art Institute of Chicago; the Hugh Lane Municipal Gallery of Modern Art, Dublin; the British Library, London and Colindale; Dr. Johnson's House Trust, London; the Garrick Club, London; Sotheby & Co., London; the Tate Gallery, London; the William Andrews Clark Memorial Library, University of California, Los Angeles; the National Gallery of Victoria, Melbourne; the Henry W. and Albert A. Berg

Collection, the New York Public Library; the Ashmolean Museum, Oxford; and the Robert H. Taylor Collection, Princeton University Library, Princeton, N. J.

Finally I must express my debt to the following publishers and authors for permission to quote from works in which they hold copyright: William Blackwood and Sons Ltd., Edinburgh and London, for "The Magic of Max," by Guy Boas; Brandt & Brandt, New York, Random House, Inc., Alfred A Knopf, Inc., New York, and Hamish Hamilton Ltd., London, for *Portrait of Max (Conversation with Max)*, by S. N. Behrman; Cambridge University Press, London, for *Lytton Strachey*, by Max Beerbohm; Lord David Cecil, and David Higham Associates Ltd., London, for *Max: A Biography*, by David Cecil; the Literary Trustees of Walter de la Mare, and the Society of Authors, London, as their representative, for "Which?" from *The Complete Poems of Walter de la Mare* (London: Faber & Faber, 1969); E. P. Dutton & Co., Inc., New York, for *And Even Now*, by Max Beerbohm (Copyright, 1921, by E. P. Dutton & Co., Inc.; renewal 1949 by Max Beerbohm); Professor Leon Edel, and Granada Publishing Ltd., London, for *Henry James: The Treacherous Years 1895-1901*, by Leon Edel; Granada Publishing Ltd., London, for *Around Theatres*, by Max Beerbohm; Sir Rupert Hart-Davis and Granada Publishing Ltd., London, for *Letters to Reggie Turner*, ed. Rupert Hart-Davis; William Heinemann Ltd., London, for *Yet Again, And Even Now*, and *Mainly on the Air*, by Max Beerbohm, and *Max Beerbohm in Perspective*, by Bohun Lynch; Macmillan, London and Basingstoke, the Macmillan Company of Canada, and the Macmillan Company, New York, for a passage from "After a Journey," from *The Collected Poems of Thomas Hardy*, by permission of the Trustees of the Hardy Estate; Martinus Nijhoff, The Hague, for *Sir Max Beerbohm, Man and Writer: A Critical Analysis with a Brief Life and a Bibliography*, by J. G. Riewald; Random House, Inc., Alfred A. Knopf, Inc., New York, for *Mainly on the Air*, by Max Beerbohm, and *Max Beerbohm in Perspective*, by Bohun Lynch; Sidgwick & Jackson Ltd., London, for "The Vagabond," from *Poems 1908-1914 by John Drinkwater*; and to various other publishers and authors, for short quotations from copyrighted material.

Among those who helped me in different ways I should particularly like to thank Sir Rupert Hart-Davis, who very kindly read an early draft of the manuscript and gave me the benefit of his expert criticism; the late Allan Wade, that distinguished bibliographer and editor; Elizabeth Anderson, lately of William Heinemann Ltd., London; Professor J. C. Arens, of the University of Nijmegen; B. J. Bradley, of the Art Institute of Chicago; Grace A. Briggs, of Harvard University Press, Cambridge, Mass.; Nancy N. Coffin, of Princeton University Library, Princeton, N. J.; William E. Conway, of the William Andrews Clark Memorial Library, Los Angeles; David Farmer, of the Humanities Research Center, University of Texas, Austin, Texas; Mrs. B. Freake, Librarian of Charterhouse School, Godalming, Surrey, England; Eleanor M. Garvey, of Harvard College Library, Cambridge, Mass.; Anne Garwood, of William Heinemann Ltd., London; Stephen and Janet Greene; the Headmaster of Charterhouse School, Godalming, Surrey, England; Professors A. G. F. van Holk and J. A. G. Tans, Dr. J. U. Terpstra, and J. A. Verleun, all of the University of Groningen, Netherlands; R. D. Mayes and M. Macfarlane, of Dr. Johnson's House Trust, London; Christine Payne, of the Birmingham Museums and Art Gallery; Cmdr. E. S. Satterthwaite, R. N., Secretary of the Garrick Club, London; Robert H. Taylor; Saundra Taylor, of the Lilly Library, Indiana University, Bloomington, Indiana; Ethna Waldron, of the Municipal Gallery of Modern Art, Dublin; Robert F. Wiseman, of the Henry W. and Albert A. Berg Collection, The New York Public Library; Irena Zdanowicz, of the National Gallery of Victoria, Melbourne; and the staffs of a variety of libraries, research institutions, and art galleries in many parts of the world, who have assisted me in this project, especially P. H. Smid, Head of the Photographic Service of the University of Groningen, under whose supervision the reproductions from the albums were made. Finally, but overwhelmingly, I am indebted to all those authors whose books I have substantially drawn upon.

University of Groningen
Netherlands

J. G. Riewald

Abbreviations

The following abbreviations have been used in referring to Max Beerbohm's writings:

AEN — *And Even Now*. London: William Heinemann, 1922 [1st ed. 1920].

AT — *Around Theatres*. London: Rupert Hart-Davis, 1953 [1st ed. 1924].

CG — *A Christmas Garland woven by Max Beerbohm*. London: William Heinemann, 1922 [1st ed. 1912; new ed. 1950].

LRT — *Letters to Reggie Turner*, ed. Rupert Hart-Davis. London: Rupert Hart-Davis, 1964.

LS — *Lytton Strachey*. The Rede Lecture 1943. Cambridge University Press, 1943.

LT — *Last Theatres, 1904-1910*, introd. Rupert Hart-Davis. London: Rupert Hart-Davis, 1970.

M — *More*. London: William Heinemann, 1922 [1st ed. 1899].

MA — *Mainly on the Air*. London: William Heinemann, 1957 [new enl. ed.; 1st ed. 1946].

MT — *More Theatres, 1898-1903*, introd. Rupert Hart-Davis. London: Rupert Hart-Davis, 1969.

MV — *Max in Verse: Rhymes and Parodies by Max Beerbohm*, ed. J. G. Riewald. Foreword by S. N. Behrman. Brattleboro, Vt.: Stephen Greene Press, 1963, and London: William Heinemann, 1964.

MW *Max and Will: Max Beerbohm and William Rothenstein, Their Friendship and Letters, 1893-1945*, ed. Mary M. Lago and Karl Beckson. London: John Murray, 1975.

PP *A Peep into the Past and other Prose Pieces by Max Beerbohm*, ed. Rupert Hart-Davis. London: William Heinemann, 1972.

SM *Seven Men*. London: William Heinemann, 1922 [1st ed. 1919].

VT *A Variety of Things*. London: William Heinemann, 1928.

W *The Works of Max Beerbohm*. London: William Heinemann, 1922 [1st ed. 1896].

YA *Yet Again*. London: William Heinemann, 1922 [1st ed. 1909].

Other abbreviations used in the text:

HD Hart-Davis, Rupert, comp. *A Catalogue of the Caricatures of Max Beerbohm*. London: Macmillan, and Cambridge, Mass.: Harvard University Press, 1972.

SC *Catalogue of the Library and Literary Manuscripts of the late Sir Max Beerbohm*. Illustrated edition. London: Sotheby & Co., 1960.

Note: *In these last two books numbers refer to catalogue entries and not to pages.*

Introduction

Sir Max Beerbohm was a dual genius who, like Blake, Dante Gabriel Rossetti, and Whistler, expressed himself through two media. He was not only a brilliant writer, but also a witty caricaturist and a master of the *portrait chargé*. For over a third of a century he has repeatedly explored and recorded the illuminating gesture, the intriguing psychological situation, the idiosyncratic stance, to create an unforgettable gallery of celebrated personalities.

Beerbohm started drawing and painting at the age of six, finding it more pleasurable than writing: writing always was uphill work for him, drawing a recreation. He never attended an art school. His first, and only, drawing lessons he got from Mrs. Wilkinson, the wife of Mr. Wilkinson, whose day school in Orme Square, London, he attended from 1881 to 1885. Later, when he was at Charterhouse, it was especially his form master Alexander Hay Tod who encouraged him to draw caricatures; sponsored by him, he completed a series of impudent caricatures of his teachers. Some of these early drawings were published in the *Greyfriar,* a school periodical, between 1887 and 1890.

Ignoring the great tradition of English caricature, the young Beerbohm invented a style of his own, of which spontaneity and skill, not perfection, was a hallmark. As Bevis Hillier says, it was left to Max "to pare down and refine the *Vanity Fair* style into a new simplified manner which would break completely with the old tradition by which caricature was merely an adaptation (to many, an inferior one) of the academic portrait." For his lack of technical knowledge, however, Beerbohm made up greatly by a charming freedom of line, which already shows itself in his first collection of drawings, *Caricatures of Twenty-Five Gentlemen* (1896).

With some exaggeration, no doubt, a contemporary critic described the impact of this album in these words: "Twenty-five bombs dropped in Piccadilly from twenty-five Zeppelins would not have created a greater sensation." This is certainly extraordinary, the more so as Max very seldom drew from the life. As he once confided to Edmund Gosse, "no pen, no notebook, merely a mild attentive gaze." He knew practically all the people of his day worth knowing; many of them were among his friends and acquaintances, thus becoming his most eligible victims, whether they liked it or not. Yet his very personal and often ruthless drawings made him no enemies—with the one exception, perhaps, of Rudyard Kipling. This may be owing to the fact that his caricatures generally lack the element of contempt: they may be critical, or mocking, or ironic, but they are never contemptuous. *On se moque de ce qu'on aime.* Max's attitude is in accordance with his belief that a good caricature should have the power to purge the beholder of superfluous contempt of its subject. Most of his victims were even proud of being caricatured by him, and their love for Beerbohm the man was by no means diminished by the fact. In the case of his literary caricatures this is proved by the numerous presentation copies of books whose authors he had caricatured, often lovingly inscribed by them to the artist. However, in addition to his caricatures of contemporaries, Max also drew many persons, real or imaginary, belonging to the near or remote past. I am thinking of his caricatures of a number of the great men of the Victorian age; they are as penetrating as those he did of the people he knew.

The development of Beerbohm the writer and that of Max the caricaturist run on parallel lines, and each may, on occasion, throw light on the other. Though he disapproved of the illustration of literary texts, he often supplied his own drawings with exquisitely apt and elaborate captions and legends. His later caricature volumes especially contain numerous examples of this rare combination of visual and verbal artistry, to such an extent even that it is sometimes difficult to say whether the legend illustrates the drawing or the other way round (as, for instance, in plate 81, "Mr. Henry James revisiting America," and plate 82, "London in November, and Mr. Henry James in London"). This complementarity of the two media is not only found in his drawings of single figures but also in those in which he reanimates or invents situations and incidents showing the subtle psychological and literary relationships between two or more people. "The truth is," Edmund Wilson writes, "that Max is quite complex, and that complexity and the intelligence it generates are what—given his double talent, a complexity in itself—have made him interesting beyond what one might expect from work that seems at first sight so playful."

Between 1896 and 1931 "the incomparable Max," as Bernard Shaw called him, published ten volumes of cartoons and caricatures. These albums represent only a fraction of his total output, which was quite considerable. The originals of his drawings are now scattered far and wide, in museums, art galleries, university libraries, and private collections; the albums themselves have not only been out of print for many years, but have themselves become collectors' items.

A distinction should here be made between Beerbohm's *cartoons* and his *caricatures*. Most of the cartoons are political or sociological in nature. They are often lethal comments on democracy, Labour, imperialism, the shape of things to come, hypocrisy and complacency, and on various kinds of political, social, and intellectual humbug. They were enjoyed by the elite of his day, though some of them are uncannily relevant to our present troubles. Beerbohm's caricatures, on the other hand, generally deal with celebrated "statesmen" (as he loved to call them), poets, writers, men of letters, artists, philosophers, public and social figures, and other outstanding personalities, both dead and alive. As might be expected, the caricatures that have survived best are those representing literary subjects. While today not many people will remember even the names of such politicians as the Earl of Rosebery, Sir William Harcourt, or Henry Chaplin (those once famous men who deemed it an honor to be a target for Max's rapier-sharp pencil), the great writers and poets are, in a very real sense, still with us. Beerbohm's perceptive caricatures of literary figures, often with his own superbly written captions and parodies, are among his best and most enduring graphic work.

Being a criticism of literature, Max's literary caricatures merit careful scrutiny by literary students; a study in depth of these drawings is bound to promote a better understanding of the men and women who actually wrote the literature, of the situation in which they found themselves, and of their problems and interrelationships. They are a salutary complement to an all too exclusive concern with their writings, and nothing but the writings. In this perspective the study of these drawings may contribute, however modestly, to the humanization of the study of literature, more particularly the literature of England between 1860 and 1920, since this period is best covered by them. It would seem, therefore, that the publication of a small, but representative selection of Max's caricatures of famous English and American poets, writers, and other men of letters—Shakespeare, Dr. Johnson, Wordsworth, Tennyson, Browning, Matthew Arnold, Whitman, Henry

James, Hardy, Conrad, George Moore, Bernard Shaw, H. G. Wells, Arnold Bennett, Yeats, and many lesser ones—with a sprinkling of "foreigners," might not be amiss.

With respect to some of his best graphics it may be said that Max drew his peculiar power from a habitual backward-looking perspective. As Osbert Lancaster remarked in his introduction to *Max's Nineties,* Beerbohm's most fruitful inspirations derived from the "backward glance"; or, as he himself once put it, "It is to the Past that I have ever had recourse from the Present." In *The Poets' Corner* (1904) he had ranged back as far as Homer, Omar Khayyám, and Dante; in *Rossetti and His Circle* (1922) he had explored the eighteen-fifties and -sixties. Yet the contemporary literary scene also held a powerful fascination for him, especially if it could be confronted with the past (as in that brilliant series of drawings entitled "The Old and the Young Self," published in *Observations* in 1925), and provided the subjects came up to his own high standard: "To be interesting," he once wrote, "a man must be complex and elusive."

Early in his career Max had defined the most perfect caricature as "that which, on a small surface, with the simplest means, most accurately exaggerates, to the highest point, the peculiarities of a human being, at his most characteristic moment, in the most beautiful manner." Thirty years later the artist in him began to realize that he was no longer seeing people in terms of caricature, but that he was seeing them as they were, was tending to make pleasant likenesses, straight portraits, of them instead of caricatures. The element of "reverence," which in his prefatory letter to *Observations* he had regarded as essential in a caricaturist, had become too strong, and consequently he decided to stop.

According to Gombrich and Kris, "the comic artist has the great advantage of being readily understood by his contemporary public." This remark, however, cannot be said to apply to Beerbohm's caricatures: they were not, as a rule, readily understood by the average contemporary public, but appealed to a cultural elite only. With respect to later generations of viewers, the situation appears to be entirely different and more complex, especially as far as his literary caricatures are concerned. Some of the writers drawn by him, such as Kipling and Bennett, are less popular now than they were in their own day; consequently caricatures of them tend to be more "difficult" for the present-day viewer. Other writers, such as James and Conrad, have gained in reputation; their works are studied in colleges and universities all over the world, with the result that caricatures of them are now more readily intelligible to comparatively large sections of the reading public than they were fifty, or sixty, or seventy years ago. Leonard Raven-Hill, the *Punch* cartoonist, was right when, in his introduction to Beerbohm's first collection of drawings, he wrote: "Max's caricatures are difficult to the public at large . . . partly because, in many cases, it is not well acquainted with the person caricatured." In spite of the widening interest in literature, what W. H. Auden said of literary parodies is equally true of literary caricatures: "Literary parodies can never appeal to more than a limited and highly sophisticated public, for they can be appreciated only by a reader who is intimately acquainted with the authors parodied." Beerbohm himself was aware of this difficulty when, in his prefatory note to *Rossetti and His Circle,* he wondered whether the public had ever heard of Rossetti, who, in his own opinion, was one of the three most interesting Englishmen of the nineteenth century—the other two being Byron and Disraeli.

I myself once, in an article on "Parody as Criticism," advanced a tentative hypothesis about the critical function of parody, an art in which Beerbohm excelled. I pointed out that the highest kind of parody might be defined as a humorous and aesthetically satisfying composition in prose or verse, usually written without malice, in which, by means of a rigidly controlled distortion, the most striking peculiarities of the subject matter and style of a literary work, or a school or type of writing, are exaggerated in such a way as to lead to an implicit value judgment of the original; and I suggested that, by its very nature, the highest kind of parody is also one of the most exacting of critical techniques.

Much of what I then wrote of parody also holds for the highest kind of caricature. Apart from the fact that the object of parody and literary criticism is the literary work itself, whereas the object of literary caricature, being a kind of biographical and psychological criticism, is the personality of the author, parody and literary caricature have much in common; with Max Beerbohm they are sometimes found side by side in one and the same drawing.

First of all, unlike literary criticism proper, parody and literary caricature are, in a superficial sense at least, not exactly true to their subject. They are fictitious models larger than life which, through exaggeration and distortion, reveal more succinctly the typical verbal and psychological idiosyncrasies of an author than could any "objective" literary or psychological analysis. It is not too much to say that, in this respect at least, literary caricature gains an advantage over literary criticism proper. It is intuitive and impressionistic rather than academic or judicial, "shorthand" for what the academic or judicial critic must write out at length. It is also more efficient, and often more effective, than literary criticism proper because by exposing through ironic mockery certain inadequate aspects of an author, it enables one to see his or her characteristic peculiarities or weaknesses simultaneously, in a flash, as it were. This does not mean, however, that the literary caricaturist lacks a clear-cut point of view, a personal stance. A good caricature illuminates a situation, poses a problem, or expresses an opinion. While exaggerating certain conspicuous features of his subject, the ideal caricaturist keeps his own distinct individuality as, what Beerbohm himself called, a "needful" point of view, without, however, obtruding himself on the viewer. It is from the juxtaposition of these two elements that true insight is born.

Another important parallel between literary caricature and parody is that, being a type of oblique or implicit criticism, literary caricature, like parody, demands a much higher degree of cooperation between artist and viewer than ordinary literary criticism does. For the graphic artist addresses himself to a person whom he regards as capable of grasping subtleties, of contributing intelligently to the act of translating into direct insights what he, the caricaturist, only implied. He elicits his viewer's aid in completing the intended critical meaning of the drawing in hand. He creates a new reality by exaggerating and distorting his original, but he expects his viewer to be able to recreate the reality from whence he departed and to achieve intellectual and aesthetic satisfaction, not only from doing so, but also from comparing the two realities. This means that the literary caricaturist can only hope to appeal to a highly educated and critically perceptive minority, and that, unlike the ordinary literary critic, he remains at least partially unintelligible to those who do not share his knowledge and intelligence.

But perhaps the most interesting similarity between literary caricature and parody on the one hand, and literary criticism proper on the other, is that literary caricature, like parody, is a kind of "Criticism without Tears." It is a *delightful* form of criticism because it is capable of disguising the critical effort in wit. Some of the amusement derived from a successful literary caricature undoubtedly lies in the sheer fun of looking at its beauties of line and color, apart from its inherent criticism. (Where the legend alone would be insufficient as an inducement to laughter, the drawing acts as a catalyst.) The laughter thus caused is purely aesthetic, i. e., removed from a personal consideration of the subject except as he reveals himself through the exaggeration of his salient points. By raising a harmless laugh, the literary caricaturist contributes to the business of criticism a lightness of tone and an atmosphere of fun which enable the critic in him to escape the imputation of too great seriousness. To be sure, any attempt to introduce a lighter tone into the criticism of literature ought to be encouraged.

While most of Beerbohm's literary caricatures are about the idiosyncrasies of individual authors and their interrelationships rather than about schools, or movements, or styles of writing, there is one group of drawings dealing exclusively with an important movement in art and literature—the Pre-Raphaelite Movement. Most of these drawings were done during the First World War, when Max lived at Far Oakridge, Stroud, Gloucestershire. Eighteen of them were shown at the Leicester Galleries, London, in September 1921, under the title "Rossetti and His Friends"; they were published in 1922 in the album *Rossetti and His Circle.* The original watercolors, formerly owned by Hugh Walpole, are now in the Tate Gallery, London.

Dante Gabriel Rossetti must have had a peculiar fascination for Max, not only because of the alien element in him—Beerbohm's own ancestors were of mixed German, Dutch, and Lithuanian origin—but also because Rossetti expressed himself in two media and used both arts to reinforce each other; like Beerbohm, he was an ambidextrous genius. Max's Rossetti drawings find their inspiration in the romantic Rossetti legend propagated by Hall Caine and Watts-Dunton, a legend which, according to Oswald Doughty, coeditor of the *Letters of Dante Gabriel Rossetti,* fostered the image of "a darkly brooding, mysterious, mystical, poet recluse, a Byronic hero who was also a *Vates Sacer,* a Poet-Seer." But the publication of these letters and of the correspondence between Rossetti and Jane Morris has destroyed this idealized, public image of the poet-painter and revealed to us a man who, in William Michael Rossetti's words, was "full of vigour and buoyancy, full of *élan,* well alive to the main chance, capable of enjoying the queer as well as the grave aspects of life, by no means behindhand in contributing his quota to the cause of high spirits—and generally a man equally natural and genial." Whereas for Dante Gabriel Rossetti the eighteen-fifties and -sixties probably had no romance at all, they were very romantic for Max, "partly," he says, "because I wasn't alive in them, and partly because Rossetti was." For him, Rossetti still shone with "the ambiguous light of a red torch somewhere in a dense fog," as he had shone for the men and women who knew him. For Max the caricaturist the as yet unexploded Rossetti myth was a godsend because it enabled him, with uncanny insight, to insinuate the hidden tensions and ambiguities that existed in Rossetti's circle. What makes this group of drawings so superior is the artist's comic treatment of the accepted, romanticized picture of Rossetti and his associates. And though Beerbohm's only material aids had been old drawings and paintings, early photographs, and the accounts of eye-witnesses, a comparison with the reproductions of Rossetti's paintings and drawings in Virginia Surtees's magnificent *Catalogue Raisonné* shows that his portraits are strikingly authentic.

In his study *The Pre-Raphaelite Imagination 1848-1900* John Dixon Hunt has explored the various modes of the literary and artistic imagination of the Pre-Raphaelites from the formation of the "Brotherhood" in 1848 through the work of later associates—Morris, Burne-Jones, Swinburne, Pater, among others—to the magazines of the 1890s, notably *The Yellow Book, The Savoy, The Dome, The Hobby Horse,* and *The Pageant.* (Beerbohm contributed to three of these.) He argues that the Pre-Raphaelite legacy to the 1890s has been unduly neglected and is as important as the more obvious French influences with which it merged. The link between Pre-Raphaelitism and aestheticism, or art for art's sake, is Edward Burne-Jones; the line of descent, according to Cecil Y. Lang, is visible and easily recognizable—Rossetti to Burne-Jones to Wilde and Beardsley, etc.; or, as Robert D. Johnston puts it, "the *Yellow Book* echoed [the voices of the Pre-Raphaelites] in the art of Aubrey Beardsley and in the writings of George Moore, Max Beerbohm, and Ernest Dowson." The fact that the influence of Rossetti's art, with its aesthetic and emotional emphasis, reached into Beerbohm's own world must have acted as an additional stimulus to his critical interest in him and his circle.

Beerbohm's own relationship with the Aesthetes and Decadents of the 1890s is not easy to define. A clue to this problem may be found in the fact that, for obvious reasons, the young Beerbohm failed to convince the reading public of the "satirical" intention of his *Yellow Book* essays, particularly "A Defence of Cosmetics." The method employed in this essay is chameleonic, and therefore ambiguous. Being a parody of Oscar Wilde and a burlesque of Walter Pater, it consists in an almost complete assimilation with the central idea and, to a lesser extent, with the stylistic peculiarities of his victims—an assimilation which is sometimes almost indistinguishable from total identification. It is this assimilation, or identification, with his subject that enables Beerbohm, as an insider, to accentuate its salient lines, so that the result is a subtle caricature in prose. But it must be insisted that this caricature is of a very special nature. From his own ambiguous attitude to a matter and a style with which, in his heart of hearts, he more or less sympathized (caricature, he believed, was a blend of mockery *and reverence,* especially "when the revered personage is of the over-serious sort"), it follows that these early essays are, in more than one sense, a reflection of the author himself. The arabesque style and vocabulary of "A Defence of Cosmetics" were not entirely due to Wilde or Pater, nor was the subject matter uncongenial to the Beerbohm of 1894. The essay has the double distinction of showing us where Beerbohm's sympathies really lay, and of giving us a covert and witty criticism of those very sympathies. In other words, it is more than a criticism of the Aesthetic Movement; it is also self-criticism.

Scholars have shown that Beerbohm's early work was influenced by the writings of Oscar Wilde. However, the exact nature of this influence is difficult to assess. It ranges from unconscious and conscious imitation to pastiche to parody, overt or veiled, or even unconscious, and it may affect either the subject matter, or the style, or both. Yet it was Oscar the man rather than Wilde the author that fascinated Max. He always praised Wilde's writings (with the exception of *Salomé,* which he thought "too horrible for definite and corporeal presentment"), and, as David Cecil remarks, this is all the stranger when we remember that Beerbohm's own style is notable for precisely the merits that Wilde's lacked: subtlety, precision, distinction. But Max was invariably amused by Oscar's gaiety, daring, and wit. According to Felstiner, he seems to have moved easily within the small London circle of homosexuals, made up of Wilde, Alfred Douglas, Robert Ross, Reggie Turner, and others, though he was not intimate with any of them, except Reggie Turner. Two years before the Wilde trials in 1895 Beerbohm wrote a satirical fantasy about him entitled "A Peep into the Past." The essay was intended for the first number of *The Yellow Book,* but held over to make way for "A Defence of Cosmetics." Its only appearance during Beerbohm's lifetime was in an unauthorized American edition of 1923, and it was not officially published until 1972, sixteen years after the author's death. The essay, a delicate, good-natured satire, represents the arch-Decadent as a domesticated old gentleman, while hinting unmistakably at the abnormal nature of Oscar's amours; but, as Cecil says, "it does so in a light-hearted tone, and with no suggestion of moral disapproval."

The Wilde trials took place at the Old Bailey in May 1895. One of Max's caricatures of Oscar (the one reproduced in plate 54) was used as evidence against the accused. Beerbohm attended the second trial; his reaction to it he records in a letter to his friend Reggie Turner: "Oscar has been quite superb. His speech about the Love that dares not tell his name was simply wonderful, and carried the whole court right away, quite a tremendous burst of applause." We know that Beerbohm himself was not averse from joking about pederasty. On 23 August 1898, a year after Wilde was released from prison, he wrote to Reggie: "Please give [Ross] some mulierastic equivalent for my love"—"mulierastic" being Ross's term for heterosexual. We also know that, while showing no moral disapproval of homosexuality, he yet tried to curb his friend Turner's inclination. On Wilde's death in 1900, Max wrote Turner: "I am, as you may imagine, very sorry indeed; and am thinking very much about Oscar, who was such an influence and an interest in my life." Many years later he protested against Frank Harris's "raking-up of the old Sodomitic cesspool" around Wilde. We may agree with Felstiner when he concludes that "Wilde's trial and imprisonment troubled but did not threaten Beerbohm; there was no complicity." There is no evidence whatever that Beerbohm was a homosexual himself.

Because in literary caricature, as in parody, the critic's point of view is implied, not overtly stated, it requires, as we have seen, a well informed and intelligent viewer, a viewer, that is, with an acute imagination and both the ability and information necessary to complete the implied meaning. Of course the ideal caricaturist will provide his viewer with a minimum of factual clues. This is what Max generally does in his literary caricatures. What strikes one in these drawings is the complexity, the utter precision and historical accuracy of these clues; they form the indispensable basis of solid fact on which the fantasy is built. "The figure may look like bisque, but the pedestal is rock." This is what a reviewer once wrote of Beerbohm's novel *Zuleika Dobson,* but it equally applies to his caricatures.

That some of Max's drawings of literary men have become familiar through frequent reproduction does not necessarily mean that they are easily understood. For the drawings to yield their full measure of enjoyment it is essential for the viewer to understand every detail of the scene, including its background and pervading ambience. In other words, his grasp of the total meaning of the drawing depends on his stock of knowledge at hand. After the lapse of so many years since the caricatures were first exhibited or published, the difficulty has certainly not lessened. Moreover, with one single exception, all the persons represented in the drawings I have selected are dead now; and though many of them belonged to the Giant Race before the Flood, they are separated from the present generation by the almost impassable gap of two World Wars.

From this it follows that, for the average modern viewer, most of these graphics require a considerable amount of explanation. In order to enjoy them, he must be able to see them in their full contemporary context. Therefore facts pertaining to biographical, literary, sociocultural, and textual matters have to be provided; persons, places, books, allusions, and so on have to be identified; particular situations have to be recreated and elucidated. It is the annotator's task to enable the viewer to participate in the artist's vision by supplying him with the materials with which to reconstruct the critical point of the drawings, and, where necessary, by analyzing on the deep structure level the exact source of the point. This is what I have tried to do in my detailed discussions and explanatory notes.

Because one caricature is more "difficult" than another, the drawings have not been treated uniformly in this respect: each commentary (found on the page facing the drawing), has been geared to the needs of the average educated viewer. To give one example only, a drawing like "Mr. Henry James" (plate 80) requires more explanation than, say, the familiar "Lord Byron, shaking the dust of England from his shoes" (plate 8). My sole aim has always been to supply the viewer with all the information he needs for a full understanding and enjoyment of the drawings I have chosen. With that kind of background they can become very much a part of the literary history of the period. For the rest, "the drawings must mostly speak for themselves," as Max wrote to Sir Rupert Hart-Davis in 1955 on being asked whether he would contribute a few notes about some of the subjects for *Max's Nineties.* My only hope is that by limiting the editorial comment to what is absolutely essential I have not deprived the viewer of one of his most inalienable rights: the unique experience of discovering the point of the drawings himself.

A special feature of the descriptive and analytical notes accompanying the graphics is the introduction of Beerbohm's own writings as a help to a fuller understanding of them. Since it has been my aim throughout this book to show the relationship between the spirit of Max's drawing and that of his writing, or even the complete fusion of his graphic and verbal imaginations, I have, wherever feasible, illustrated the drawings with the artist's own words. Other significant parts of the explanatory and critical comment have been contributed by his biographers and critics and by myself. I trust that in doing so I have succeeded in achieving an interesting confrontation of Beerbohm's own views with those of his students.

A word should be said here concerning the principle underlying my selection of the drawings. Sir Rupert Hart-Davis, in his *Catalogue of the Caricatures of Max Beerbohm,* records a total of 2,093 items, of which only 341 are reproduced in the ten albums published by Max himself: *Caricatures of Twenty-Five Gentlemen* (1896), *The Poets'*

Corner (1904), *A Book of Caricatures* (1907), *Cartoons "The Second Childhood of John Bull"* (1911), *Fifty Caricatures* (1913), *A Survey* (1921), *Rossetti and His Circle* (1922), *Things New and Old* (1923), *Observations* (1925), and *Heroes and Heroines of Bitter Sweet* (1931). Of the 105 drawings included in this book, 89 were first published in these albums. Since the albums obviously represent what was best in Max's own eyes, I have thought it my duty to do justice to the initial act of selection made by the artist himself, the more so because his judgment and taste in these matters was always faultless. Of course the purely "literary" collections have yielded a proportionally large number of items; thus, with the exception of one plate, *The Poets' Corner* has been reprinted in full, though not in its original order.

In selecting the drawings from these volumes I have tried to include as many genuine caricatures of poets, novelists, dramatists, and other men of letters as possible. However, rather than attempt to construct a sort of pictorial history of literature, it has been my aim to display the quality of the artist's literary insights wherever it is most apparent. This policy accounts for the omission of drawings that are portraits rather than caricatures, i.e., express little beyond mere physical likeness, such as those of Mark Twain (HD 1689) and George Meredith (HD 1032). Needless to say, faced as I was with an abundance of material, the choice has often been difficult; given the exigencies of space, several items which I would have liked to include have had to be omitted. However, a few of Beerbohm's "improvements," i.e., comic alterations of portraits made by others, have been included for good measure (plates 27, 72, 79). Forty-eight of the drawings have been reproduced from the originals in public collections and institutions; the others, being in private hands and therefore difficult to trace, have been reproduced from my own copies of the albums, from the Sotheby catalogue (plate 72), or, as in the case of the "improved" Tolstoy portrait (plate 79), from the original in my possession.

For practical reasons I have found it expedient to arrange the drawings under the following, somewhat arbitrary, headings: Poets, Playwrights, Essayists, Rossetti and His Circle, Aesthetes and Decadents, A Variety of Writers, Novelists. With an arrangement of this kind a certain amount of overlapping was, of course, inevitable, since many of the authors caricatured excelled in more than one literary field. In placing them in their most appropriate categories I have naturally been guided by the aspect under which Max himself treats them. Thus "Mr. Thomas Hardy composing a lyric" (plate 13) is ranged with the poets, not with the novelists. Within each of these categories the drawings have been arranged in a roughly chronological order. Because some of the persons caricatured occur in more than one drawing, cross-references have been provided throughout. An Index of Persons Caricatured has been added for facility of access and reference.

Since all the drawings in this book are reproduced in black and white, many of them, except the line drawings, have inevitably lost much of their original brilliance and subtlety. As Rupert Hart-Davis says in his *Catalogue*, "Max was primarily a water-colour artist, and the full effect of his drawings can be seen only in the originals: black-and-white reproductions convey the joke and the draughtsmanship only." Most of the graphics have also been reduced in size, with the result that the true proportions have been disturbed and the beautifully written captions and legends have become almost illegible.

It will be noted that, in a few instances, there exists some slight discrepancy between the text written on the drawing and Beerbohm's own printed version of it in the published albums. Thus, when the caricature entitled "Re-appearance of Mr. George Moore in Chelsea" (plate 90) was published, Max, besides making one or two minor changes in the text, replaced the word "Re-appearance," which occurs in the title of the drawing, by "Rentrée" in the letterpress accompanying it in *Fifty Caricatures*. In this case, as in a few similar cases, I have reproduced the printed text, as I have done throughout the book. Representing as it does the artist's last thoughts on the matter—Beerbohm was quite meticulous in revising his proofs—the printed text may be considered to be the definitive one; however, major variants of it written on the drawings have been duly recorded. (The only exception is plate 43, where I have printed the fuller version written on the drawing.) The listings on the half-title pages are generally those used by Max himself in the tables of contents of his albums. The descriptions and analyses contain an indication of the source of the reproduction (either one of the albums, the original drawing, or some other source), the (conjectural) date of the drawing, and, wherever applicable, its number in the Hart-Davis catalogue. With respect to the dating I have followed the practice adopted in this catalogue: a plain date, preceded by a period, means that Max wrote it on the drawing; [n. d.] means that the drawing is undated; dates within square brackets are conjectural. The words "right" and "left" refer to the right and left of the drawing as seen by the spectator.

Part One

Poets

1. Homer
2. Omar Khayyám
3. Dante
4. Goethe
5. Robert Burns
6. William Wordsworth
7. Samuel Taylor Coleridge
8. Lord Byron
9. Alfred, Lord Tennyson
10. Woolner at Farringford
11. Robert Browning
12. Walt Whitman
13. Thomas Hardy
14. Paul Verlaine
15. Paderewski and D'Annunzio
16. John Masefield
17. John Drinkwater

1 Homer, the first poet in the Western world, must have lived between 1100 and 850 B.C. Of his parentage and birth nothing is known with certainty. His authorship of the two great epics, the *Iliad* and the *Odyssey,* was first questioned by the German scholar Friedrich Adolf Wolf, who tried to show that "the two epics were not the work of one man but a compilation of popular lays and poems by a multitude of early poets. This led to a violent academic controversy, known as 'The Homeric Question,' which raged for a century and a half and which still continues although its virulence has subsided. . . . Today the consensus of the vast majority of Homeric scholars is that the epics were written by one man" (Michalopoulos, pp. 32-33, 34).

The drawing is a humorous illustration of the nineteenth-century dispute over the poet's identity. It shows a many-headed Homer, deprived of his identity and of his works, strumming a lyre and reduced to beggary. The multiple heads represent the various poets to whom his works have been attributed; the ship suggests the long wanderings of Odysseus, the Greek hero and king of Ithaca, described in the *Odyssey.* According to an old Greek tradition, Homer was blind. If so, he may have lost his sight late in life. The Greek inscription on the board hanging on the poet's breast means *blind.*

A verbal equivalent of the problem illustrated in this drawing is found in Beerbohm's remark about King George IV: "We know he was fond of quoting those incomparable poets, Homer, at great length" (*W,* p.80).

Homer, going his round [1904]
The Poets' Corner (1904)
HD 766

1

2 Omar Khayyám, the Persian mathematician, astronomer, freethinker, and epigrammatist, was born at Níshápúr, Iran, in the latter half of the eleventh century, and died within the first quarter of the twelfth century.

Edward FitzGerald's very unliteral translation of the *Rubáiyát of Omar Khayyám* was first published in 1859. It was received enthusiastically by the Pre-Raphaelites and became extremely popular in Victorian England both for its musicality and for its doubts on religion. During the nineties the faintly decadent ring of its quatrains fell in with the current gospel of art for art's sake. New editions appeared in rapid succession. For the year 1904 only, the year in which Max's drawing was published, the British Museum Catalogue lists as many as nine reprints. Beerbohm owned a copy of an 1898 edition (SC 166).

In his drawing Max ridicules the romantic self-indulgence of FitzGerald's *Rubáiyát*: "Omar, so fat that he must be shown lying down, reads from a tiny pink book numbered one. Other items in the famous stanza are duly identified by number: the bough, loaf of bread, jug of wine, Thou (an unattractive female yawning in neglect), and 'Wilderness,' the endless monotonous desert" (McElderry 1968, p. 81).

The caricature illustrates the text of quatrain XII of the fourth edition of FitzGerald's translation, published in 1879:

> A Book of Verses underneath the Bough,
> A Jug of Wine, a Loaf of Bread—and Thou
> Beside me singing in the Wilderness—
> Oh, Wilderness were Paradise enow!

The inscription on the drawing reads: (1 - Book of Verses
2 - Bough
3 - Loaf of Bread
4 - Jug of Wine
5 - Thou
6 - Wilderness).

Omar Khayyám [1904]
The Poets' Corner (1904)
HD 847

2

3 During a nocturnal stroll through Oxford, "dour Dante"—Beerbohm's phrase (*AEN*, p. 142)—is interrogated by a Proctor, who asks him the usual question: "Your name and college?" At Oxford a Proctor is a high university official elected annually to discharge various important functions, including the duty of inquiring into and reporting on any breaches of the university's statutes, customs, or privileges, the maintenance of discipline among students, and the summary punishment of minor offenses. The two figures behind the Proctor are the sworn constables, familiarly known as "bulldogs," who accompany him in his nightly perambulation of the streets for the purpose of preventing disorder. The building in the background looks like an evocation of Beerbohm's own college, Merton.

The drawing may have been inspired by a meeting of the members of the Dante Society, held at the City of London College on 9 February 1893, at which the Rev. H. P. Gurney read a lecture by William Ewart Gladstone, the English statesman and author, entitled "Did Dante study in Oxford?" According to the lecturer, external and corroborative evidence pointed to the conclusion that he did. Beerbohm was then an Oxford undergraduate and he must have heard about the meeting and its proceedings. Gladstone's lecture was published in *The Dante Society Lectures*, vol. III (London: The "Pall Mall" Press, 1909), pp. 19-41.

One of the best critical editions of Dante Alighieri's complete works is the revised edition of the Oxford Dante (1924), originally published by Paget Toynbee in 1894, and reprinted by the Oxford University Press in 1895, 1897, 1904, and 1914. The quick succession of reprints is an indication of the tremendous interest in Dante during the nineties and following years. Max's caricature was probably drawn in 1904; it may have been occasioned by the publication of the 1904 Oxford edition.

On 21 June 1902 Beerbohm reviewed F. Marion Crawford's play *Francesca da Rimini*, and on 9 May 1903 Victorien Sardou's play *Dante* (*MT*, pp. 474-77, 565-69). In the latter article he referred to Dante's face in these words: "We do not know exactly what Dante looked like. There is the death-mask of him, quite authentic. For bronze substitute flesh and blood, and lo! there, quite authentic, is the fine face of Sir Henry

Dante in Oxford [1904]
The Poets' Corner (1904)
HD 402

3

PROCTOR: "Your name and college?"

Irving. The only difference is that Dante's upper-lip is a trifle shorter. 3
But what is true of noses is not true of upper-lips" (p. 566). Beerbohm's remark about Dante's and Irving's noses is confirmed by his caricature entitled "A Memory of Henry Irving," dated 1926 (the twenty-first anniversary of the death of the famous actor-manager), and reproduced in *Caricatures by Max* (No. 7). The resemblance between their noses is indeed striking.

4 Lili, the woman celebrated in a few of Goethe's lyrics, was Anna Elisabeth Schönemann (1758-1817), to whom Goethe was for a time engaged in 1774-75. She was the daughter of Johann Wolfgang Schönemann, one of the foremost Frankfurt bankers. Goethe ran away from her in the autumn of 1775, not because of the family opposition between the Calvinist Schönemanns and the Lutheran Goethes, but because of Goethe's dedication to love in general, rather than to some particular individual. Three years later Lili married the Strasbourg banker Bernhard Friedrich von Türckheim.

The drawing is a comic illustration of a passage like the following from Johann Wolfgang Goethe, "An Lili," *Sämtliche Gedichte,* vol. II, p. 229:

> Im holden Tal, auf schneebedeckten Höhen
> War stets dein Bild mir nah;
> Ich sah's um mich in lichten Wolken wehen,
> Im Herzen war mir's da.
>
> In the lovely vale, on the snowy hills
> Your image was always near me;
> I saw it floating around me in light clouds,
> I carried it in my heart.

Beerbohm's interest in Goethe also appears from his essay "Quia Imperfectum" (*AEN,* pp. 193-212), a mocking psychological study in depth of the relations between Goethe and his friend Johann Heinrich Wilhelm Tischbein. The essay centers around Tischbein's most famous portrait, "Goethe in the Campagna," painted in 1787 when the two men traveled from Rome to Naples.

Goethe, watching the shadow of Lili on the blind [1904]
The Poets' Corner (1904)
HD 598

4

5 The real name of Burns's "Highland Mary" was Mary Campbell, the eldest daughter of Archibald Campbell, a sea-captain. She was born at Dunoon, on the right bank of the river Clyde, in 1764, and died in the autumn of 1786. She was buried in West Churchyard, Greenock, where a monument was erected over her grave in 1842.

"When in 1786 [Burns] fell in love with Jean Armour, her father refused to allow her to marry Burns even though a child was on the way and under Scots law mutual consent followed by consummation constituted a legal marriage. Jean was persuaded by her father to go back on her promise; Robert, hurt and enraged, took up with another girl, Mary Campbell, who died shortly afterwards; Jean bore him twins out of wedlock. Meanwhile, the farm was not prospering" (Daiches 1957, p. 17).

O pale, pale now, those rosy lips,
I aft have kiss'd sae fondly!
And closed for aye the sparkling glance,
That dwelt on me sae kindly!
And mould'ring now in silent dust,
That heart that lo'ed me dearly!
But still within my bosom's core
Shall live my Highland Mary.

From Robert Burns, "Highland Mary," *The Poetical Works of Robert Burns*, p. 320.

The drawing was inspired by Luke ix. 62: "And Jesus said unto him, No man, having put his hand to the plough, and looking back, is fit for the kingdom of God" (Authorized Version).

Robert Burns, having set his hand to the plough, looks back at Highland Mary [1904]
The Poets' Corner (1904)
HD 206

5

6

The drawing shows "a crabbed and morose old gentleman, dressed in solemn Victorian state with a towering top hat upon his head, crossly interrogating a singularly unresponsive child; while the rain pours down impartially upon the lake and the mountains in the distance and the poet and his unrewarding companion in the foreground. The chief figure appears to be the very model, one might say, of a humourless eminent Victorian. It is a picture which indicates how imprudent it is in a poet to live too long; for the boring old Victorian poet laureate satirized by Max was in fact already an old man before the Victorian era began" (Thompson).

Max's drawing may be seen as an ironic comment on Wordsworth's sonnet beginning "It is a beauteous evening, calm and free," especially on the last six lines:

> Dear Child! dear Girl! that walkest with me here,
> If thou appear untouched by solemn thought,
> Thy nature is not therefore less divine:
> Thou liest in Abraham's bosom all the year;
> And worshipp'st at the Temple's inner shrine,
> God being with thee when we know it not.

The Poetical Works of William Wordsworth, III, p. 17.

More particularly, the drawing may refer to the poet interviewing the little girl in "We are Seven."

Cf. plates 61 and 76, and Beerbohm's parodies of Wordsworth's sonnet "London, 1802" in *MV*, pp. 27 and 123.

Wordsworth in the Lake District—at cross-purposes [1904]
Courtesy of the Hugh Lane Municipal Gallery of Modern Art, Dublin
HD 1810

6

7 Coleridge's nephew, Henry Nelson Coleridge, published some specimens of the poet's table talk of the last few years—1822 to his death in 1834—under the title *Specimens of the Table Talk of the late Samuel Taylor Coleridge* (1835). The drawing may have been inspired by the following passage from H. N. Coleridge's preface: "There were, indeed, some whom Coleridge tired, and some he sent asleep. It would occasionally so happen, when the abstruser mood was strong upon him, and the visiter [*sic*] was narrow and ungenial. I have seen him at times when you could not incarnate him,—when he shook aside your petty questions or doubts, and burst with some impatience through the obstacles of common conversation. Then, escaped from the flesh, he would soar upwards into an atmosphere almost too rare to breathe, but which seemed proper to *him*, and there he would float at ease. Like enough, what Coleridge then said, his subtlest listener would not understand as a man understands a newspaper; but upon such a listener there would steal an influence, and an impression, and a sympathy; there would be a gradual attempering of his body and spirit, till his total being vibrated with one pulse alone, and thought became merged in contemplation" (pp. xvi-xvii).

In the drawing the poet sits, tirelessly discoursing, and "slightly overcome, at one end of his table, while his guests lean together on either side; so that in the front and the back view there is an almost pyramidal effect, each man leaning on his neighbour, till we come to the apex, a guest with his nose pointing upwards. They are all snoring" (Lynch, p. 128).

Samuel Taylor Coleridge, table-talking [1904]
The Poets' Corner (1904)
HD 351

7

8

On 2 January 1815 Lord Byron married Anne Isabella ("Annabella") Milbanke. The marriage was not a happy one. After the birth of a daughter, Augusta Ada, Annabella returned to her parents and obtained a legal separation on the grounds of her husband's cruelty and insanity. At the same time there were sinister whispers about Byron's incestuous relationship with his half-sister Augusta Leigh, and his homosexual tendencies. After the separation husband and wife never met again. Finding himself ostracized by the society which had previously lionized him, the poet left England for ever. He sailed from Dover for Ostend on 23 April 1816.

The words of the caption echo Matt. x.14: "And whosoever shall not receive you, nor hear your words, when ye depart out of that house or city, shake off the dust of your feet" (Authorized Version).

Beerbohm reckoned Byron among the three most interesting men that England had in the nineteenth century—the other two being Disraeli and Rossetti. "Shelley, for example, was a far finer poet than Byron. But he was not in himself interesting: he was just a crystal-clear crank. To be interesting, a man must be complex and elusive" (*Rossetti and His Circle*, p. vi).

Lord Byron, shaking the dust of England from his shoes [1904]
The Poets' Corner (1904)
HD 210

8

9 Tennyson's "In Memoriam," a poem in memory of his intimate friend Arthur H. Hallam, was written between 1833 and 1850 and published in the latter year. Five weeks before its publication, Wordsworth, the Poet Laureate, had died, and it was "In Memoriam" that caused Queen Victoria to offer the laureateship to Tennyson. She and the Prince Consort greatly admired the poem, and after Prince Albert's death in 1861 it was the only book, besides religious books, to which she turned for comfort. In 1862 the Queen wished the poet to call and see her when she was next at Osborne. The visit, which made a deep impression on the Queen, took place on 14 April.

"The sparsely furnished room of the palace, redolent of utility furniture in a boarding-house, with the two elongated fire-irons in the grate and the heraldic clock on the mantelpiece, is an irregular but lambent comment on the decorative taste of the Victorian age. The black of the widow's weeds, the sympathetic black of the poet's doublet (also his trousers and hair, together with the Bismarckian portrait of the late Prince Consort over the chimney-piece), and the irreverent query whether the widowhood, sincere as it was, was perhaps just a trifle excessive, while in the poise of the Laureate's hand, raised heavenwards as he declaims the elegy, the innocent but supernumerary query is added whether it would not be even easier to admire the transcendent qualities of the bard had not such a just estimate of them already been vouchsafed to him by his own intuition" (Boas, pp. 346-47).

In a different state of this drawing, now in the Robert H. Taylor Collection at Princeton, N. J., the wallpaper has a design of skulls and cross-bones instead of flowers; on the mount of this drawing Beerbohm has written: "For Nicholsons: William and Mabel—from Max—1904."

Beerbohm owned a copy of the 1890 edition of Tennyson's *Works,* in which he has ingeniously altered the portrait of the poet and "improved" the title-page by the addition of a printed illustration of three hilarious figures in carnival costume (SC 224).

See plate 10.

Mr. Tennyson, reading "In Memoriam" to his Sovereign [1904]
The Poets' Corner (1904)
HD 1656

9

10 Thomas Woolner (1825-92), the English sculptor and poet, and one of the original seven Pre-Raphaelite Brethren, executed a marble bust of Tennyson in 1857. Tennyson then lived at Farringford, near Freshwater, in the Isle of Wight. Before that, Woolner had executed two medallions of the Poet Laureate. The work on the bust is continually mentioned in the correspondence between Woolner and Mrs. Tennyson. On 8 March 1857 Woolner wrote her from London that the bust was finished. It is now in the library of Trinity College, Cambridge.

The two large portraits on the wall are those of Mr. and Mrs. Tennyson. The text on the drawing itself reads: "I'm the most unmeddlesome of women."

See plate 9.

Woolner at Farringford, 1857. 1917
Courtesy of the Tate Gallery, London
HD 1657

10

Mrs. Tennyson: "You know, Mr. Woolner, I'm one of the most un-meddlesome of women; but—when (I'm only asking), *when* do you begin modelling his halo?"

11

The Browning Society, inaugurated in 1881 by Dr. F. J. Furnivall, the Shakespeare editor and founder of the Early English Text Society, was the result of the growing interest in Browning's work, and helped to extend the study of it. Its members occupied themselves with unraveling the poet's obscurities, expounding his meaning, and promoting his philosophy. The poet, accepting the homage in a simple and friendly way, treated the members of the Society with ceremonious politeness, though he avoided any action which would make him responsible for the Society's Papers, edited by Furnivall from 1881 to 1891.

In the drawing, "the poet, seated on a pink-upholstered chair, is surrounded by fifteen unsmiling figures reflecting in a variety of expressions, reverence, mystification, polite boredom, and even querulous indignation. Beerbohm assumes, of course, that Browning's actual aversion to the formation of a Browning Society is known to the viewer of his drawing" (McElderry 1968, p. 81).

"About Shakespeare, and Vergil, and Goethe," Beerbohm once wrote, "we are sentimental, all of us. We do more than merely admire their work: we love them. Browning we love too. We could not have done so in the days of the Browning Society; but now Browning has emerged upon Parnassus, and there is no more of the strenuous twaddle that exasperated us" (*MT*, p. 174).

Beerbohm owned a 1907 copy of Browning's *Poems,* in which he has strangely altered the portrait, and "improved" the title-page by the addition of a Victorian woodcut in comic allusion to Browning's elopement with Elizabeth Barrett (SC 41).

Robert Browning, taking tea with the Browning Society [1904]
Courtesy of the Ashmolean Museum, Oxford
HD 187

11

12

Walt Whitman (1819-92), author of *Leaves of Grass,* was the first great American poet. Preaching the democratic virtues of liberty, fraternity, and equality, he sang of "a nation announcing itself." But the praise of the reviewers of the first (1855), privately printed, edition of *Leaves of Grass* was not unqualified. One reviewer referred to the poet as "an odd genius," another called his book "a mixture of Yankee transcendentalism and New York rowdyism." Whitman then decided that if *Leaves of Grass* was to receive further critical attention, he would have to provide the reviews himself, which he duly did.

In the drawing the poet is shown merrily performing an awkward dance in front of an unresponsive American eagle, trying to incite it to soar.

Beerbohm divided great men into two classes, the lovable and the unlovable. Like Robert Browning, Walt Whitman belonged to the class of essentially lovable men: " . . . as surely as Whitman and Browning are typical of the one class, Ibsen is typical of the other" (*AT,* p. 433).

See plates 11 and 19.

Walt Whitman, inciting the bird of freedom to soar [1904]
The Poets' Corner (1904)
HD 1776

12

13 Emma Lavinia Gifford, the first wife of Thomas Hardy (1840-1928), the English poet and novelist, died in 1912. There had been certain differences between them, and at times Emma had been subject to delusions. After her death Hardy found release and consolation in dwelling on her memory. Some of his lyrics imply that he had not always realized her predicament and that he had failed to treat her with sufficient care.

The drawing powerfully suggests the mystery of the phantom-haunted landscape of much of Hardy's poetry. The artist "gives the poet a beautifully musing expression, which is probably what [the second] Mrs. Hardy had in mind when she wrote later that Beerbohm's caricatures of her husband 'show greater insight than any other portraits'" (Felstiner 1973, p. 137). Cf. the following passage from "After a Journey," written 1912-13:

> Hereto I come to view a voiceless ghost;
> Whither, O whither will its whim now draw me?
> Up the cliff, down, till I'm lonely, lost,
> And the unseen waters' ejaculations awe me.
> Where you will next be there's no knowing,
> Facing round about me everywhere,
> With your nut-coloured hair,
> And gray eyes, and rose-flush coming and going.

The Collected Poems of Thomas Hardy, p. 328.

Beerbohm parodied Hardy's thought and style in "A Sequelula to 'The Dynasts'" (*CG*, pp. 53-66; reprinted in *MV*, pp. 36-45). See also Beerbohm's reviews of a performance of a dramatized version of *Tess of the D'Urbervilles* (*AT*, pp. 65-68) and of *The Dynasts* (*LT*, pp. 20-25), and his verses entitled "Thomas Hardy and A. E. Housman" and "A Luncheon" (*MV*, pp. 62, 118).

Mr. Thomas Hardy composing a lyric [1913]
Courtesy of Charterhouse School, Godalming, Surrey, England
HD 701

13

14 After deserting his wife, the French poet Paul Verlaine (1844-96) stayed in England for a short time, acting as a teacher, first at Stickney, Lincolnshire, where he taught French and drawing, afterwards at St. Aloysius College in Bournemouth. "St. Aloysius College, despite its high-sounding name, was a small affair. The principal, a Protestant clergyman named Remington who had been converted to Catholicism, had only about a dozen pupils. Several of these were Irish boys who, according to Verlaine, were 'real imps.' It was his duty to teach them French and classics and to take them down to the beach every day through the pine-woods to bathe" (Bechhofer Roberts, pp. 167-68). In the autumn of 1879 Verlaine was engaged as French master in Murdoch's school, Lymington, Hampshire, but this post, too, he soon gave up.

The caricature shows the poet, alcoholic and syphilitic, on one of his walks with his pupils. Instead of the date "1877-1878," the original drawing has the words "Sunday morning."

Paul Verlaine (Usher in private school at Bournemouth, 1877-1878) [1904]

The Poets' Corner (1904)

HD 1723

14

15 The title of the caption is from Ovid's *Metamorphoses*, XIV, 158: "Post taedia longa laborum": After the long tedium of work. Both Paderewski and D'Annunzio had recently been drawn from art into politics.

From 1910 Ignacy Jan Paderewski (1860-1941), the Polish pianist, composer, statesman, and patriot, was a leading advocate of the Polish national cause. Early in 1919 he formed a Polish government, but his premiership was not a success and he resigned in November of that year, after which he resumed his musical career.

Gabriele D'Annunzio (1863-1938), the Italian poet, novelist, playwright, politician, and Fascist theoretician, served in the Italian army from 1915 to 1918. With less than three hundred volunteers he seized Fiume in 1919 in order to prevent its being handed over to Yugoslavia, but in December 1920 he was expelled from it by Italian forces.

The Lilly Library, Indiana University, Bloomington, Indiana, possesses what seems to be an earlier and less perfect state of this drawing, also dated 1920.

Post Taedia Longa Laborum. 1920
A Survey (1921)
HD 401

15

M. Paderewski: "Ah, read me one of the poems of your youth!"
Signor D'Annunzio: "Ah, play me one of your adorable sonatas!"

16 John Masefield (1878-1967) succeeded Robert Bridges as Poet Laureate in 1930. Max's drawing was clearly inspired by the expletives in Masefield's long narrative poems, such as *The Everlasting Mercy* (1911) and, to a lesser extent, *Dauber* (1913). On its appearance, the former poem was criticized as obscene on account of the oaths and curses and pub and slum scenes it contained.

Beerbohm's lines are a skit on Wordsworth's *Peter Bell* (1819), I, 248-50:

> A primrose by a river's brim
> A yellow primrose was to him,
> And it was nothing more.

The Poetical Works of William Wordsworth,
II, p. 341.

In his review of Masefield's play *The Campden Wonder* (12 January 1907), Max had already criticized its dialogue, though not on grounds of obscenity: "The first of the three scenes is rather tedious, by reason of the manner of the quarrel between the brothers. 'Ye're a drunken sot, John Perry.' 'No, I bain't.' 'Yes, you be.' 'Oh, I'm a drunken sot, am I?' 'Yes, and you're a disgrace to Campden.' 'No, I bain't.' 'Yes, you be.' 'Oh, I'm a disgrace to Campden, am I?' . . . I have no doubt that this scene between John and Richard is perfectly true to life—so far as it goes. For perfect truth, I dare say, it ought to go much further. But perfect truth to life is not art" (*AT*, pp. 446-47). According to Beerbohm, Masefield's play *The Tragedy of Nan* came within the same category (*LT*, p. 374).

Beerbohm owned a presentation copy of the first edition (1930) of Masefield's *The Wanderer of Liverpool* (SC 149).

See plate 33.

Mr. John Masefield. 1913
Fifty Caricatures (1913)
HD 1018

16

A swear-word in a rustic slum
A simple swear-word is to some,
To Masefield something more.

17 This drawing of John Drinkwater (1882-1937), the English nature poet, playwright, and critic, may have been occasioned by the publication, in 1925, of his *New Poems.* It seems to epitomize the mood of a characteristic Drinkwater poem like the following:

The Vagabond

I know the pools where the grayling rise,
I know the trees where the filberts fall,
I know the woods where the red fox lies,
The twisted elms where the brown owls call.
And I've seldom a shilling to call my own,
And there's never a girl I'd marry,
I thank the Lord I'm a rolling stone
With never a care to carry.

I talk to the stars as they come and go
On every night from July to June,
I'm free of the speech of the winds that blow,
And I know what weather will sing what tune.
I sow no seed and I pay no rent,
And I thank no man for his bounties,
But I've a treasure that's never spent,
I'm lord of a dozen counties.

Poems 1908-1914 by John Drinkwater, p. 109.

Beerbohm's lines "Same Cottage—but Another Song, of Another Season" (*MV,* p. 73) are a parody of Drinkwater's "Cottage Song," a lyric memory of a summer (1917) spent in William Rothenstein's cottage at Far Oakridge, Stroud, Gloucestershire.

Max owned copies of the first English or American editions of several of Drinkwater's works, including a copy of his *New Poems,* all with authograph presentation inscriptions by the author (SC 60-62).

Mr. John Drinkwater. 1925
Observations (1925)
HD 446

17

Part Two

Playwrights

18. William Shakespeare
19. Henrik Ibsen and William Archer
20. Henry Arthur Jones
21. Arthur Wing Pinero
22. Bernard Shaw
23. Bernard Shaw and Max Beerbohm
24. Georg Brandes and G. B. S.
25. Mr. Shaw's Apotheosis
26. The Old and the Young Self: Bernard Shaw
27. The Socialist
28. J. M. Barrie
29. Gerhart Hauptmann
30. Jacques Blanche and Maurice Maeterlinck
31. Edward Martyn and W. B. Yeats
32. W. B. Yeats and George Moore
33. The British Drama
34. Noel Coward

18 In the great controversy that for more than a hundred years has raged over the authorship of the Shakespeare plays, anti-Stratfordians have variously attributed them to Francis Bacon, Edward de Vere, Seventeenth Earl of Oxford, William Stanley, Sixth Earl of Derby, Christopher Marlowe, Roger Manners, Fifth Earl of Rutland, Sir Edward Dyer, Robert Burton, and others. The drawing shows William Shakespeare being furtively handed the manuscript of *Hamlet* by Francis Bacon.

In 1903, one year before the publication of *The Poets' Corner,* Sir Walter W. Greg published his "Facts and Fancies in Baconian Theory," a reply to W. H. Mallock's "New Facts relating to the Bacon-Shakespeare Question," which had appeared earlier that year. But besides this exchange, several other books and articles dealing with this controversy were published shortly before and in 1904.

In an essay entitled, "On Shakespeare's Birthday," originally published in *The Saturday Review* (London) for 26 April 1902, Beerbohm had written: "The Baconians have . . . made themselves very ridiculous; and that alone is reason enough for not wishing to join them. And yet my heart is with them, and my voice urges them to carry on the fight," because, he continues, if they succeeded in their efforts, the plays would remain, and we would be rid of a great deal of tiresome hero-worship (*YA*, pp. 220-22).

Beerbohm succeeded Bernard Shaw as dramatic critic of *The Saturday Review* in 1898. He reviewed, between 1898 and 1910, more than thirty performances of Shakespeare's plays in various London theaters. "Though in his comments in 1898 on *Macbeth* he censured the cowardliness of Shaw's attacks on a playwright who could not defend himself, Beerbohm himself adopted essentially the same line of attack. For him, as for Shaw, the enemy was not so much Shakespeare as the stodgy tradition that had grown up around his plays. They were so much set apart from the living theater that all too often they were given reverential and undiscriminating praise" (McElderry 1972, p. 73).

See also Beerbohm's lines on "The Characters of Shakespeare" (*MV*, pp. 31-33).

William Shakespeare, his method of work [1904]
The Poets' Corner (1904)
HD 1472

18

19 Henrik Ibsen (1828-1906), the Norwegian dramatist, was an exceptionally unamiable character. In his obituary essay on the dramatist's death Beerbohm wrote: "There is something impressive, something magnificent and noble, in the spectacle of his absorption in himself—the impregnability of that rock on which his art was founded" (*AT*, pp. 433-34). However, what Beerbohm missed in him was the "capacity for friendship." Ibsen, he said, was "a hater, first and last, who loved not even himself; an unlovable man, who . . . could by no manner of means be made lovable" (Riewald 1953, p. 158).

In 1904, the year in which this drawing was probably made, Beerbohm met his future wife, the American actress Florence Kahn, who had appeared in two Ibsen plays before arriving in London. The year before, Beerbohm had reviewed a performance of Ibsen's *When We Dead Awaken* (*MT*, pp. 532-35) and *Hedda Gabler* (*AT*, pp. 277-81).

William Archer (1856-1924), the distinguished drama critic and playwright, had helped to introduce the "new drama" to the English public by his translations of the plays of Ibsen, whose collected works he edited in 1906-12. In an unsigned obituary note in *The Times* of 6 January 1925 Beerbohm said of Archer that he "was ever an indefatigably unselfish man" (*PP*, p. 53).

The caricature plays upon Ibsen's egoism and upon Archer's adoration of the master. Archer, like most translators, had an "exaggerated veneration for original authors," Beerbohm wrote in 1903 (*MT*, pp. 587-88). The drawing shows a suppliant Archer "kissing the foot of a gruff and condescending Ibsen. The pattern of Ibsen's hair and glasses is repeated on the wall paper of the room, thus accentuating the impression that Ibsen was extremely egotistic" (Stevenson, p. 84), or rather, self-infatuated. It is said that, in idle moments, Ibsen enjoyed staring at himself in a little mirror which he carried for the purpose in the crown of his top hat.

Beerbohm owned a copy of William Archer's translation of Ibsen's *When We Dead Awaken,* published in 1900 (SC 119).

See plate 33.

Henrik Ibsen, receiving Mr. William Archer in audience [1904]
Courtesy of the Hugh Lane Municipal Gallery of Modern Art, Dublin
HD 28

19

20 Henry Arthur Jones (1851-1929) played an important part in the revival of British drama. In his popular plays he satirized English hypocrisy and intolerance, Victorian prudery, the abuse of religion as a handmaid to industry, the pompousness of the Established Church, the cupidity of speculators, and the aristocratic patronage of fads. But his moral and social criticism was weakened by the fact that it lacked a firm philosophical basis.

Jones, "a vigorous-minded, warm-hearted, pugnacious man, often dressed in riding-breeches, became a real friend [of Beerbohm's]. Max enjoyed his society . . . partly because Jones was such a contrast to his fastidious self. 'He is such an entirely *natural* little man,' he once said, 'so different from Pinero [his chief rival as popular dramatist], who lives in deadly fear of being seen through'" (Cecil, pp. 129-130).

Beerbohm also admired Jones as a social moralist: "Of all successful playwrights it was Jones who was 'the most nearly in touch with actual life,' as, for instance, in that most perfect of all his plays, *The Liars,* a realistic comedy of manners . . . Jones was also, with the exception of Wilde, 'the only dramatist of any intellectual force, the only dramatist with ideas.' He possessed 'enthusiastic sympathies,' 'humanity,' 'power of satire,' and 'vitality.' He could, moreover, tell a story on the stage, and, as in his music-hall sketch *The Knife,* come quickly to the point; in brief, he was an unrivalled craftsman" (Riewald 1953, p. 155).

Beerbohm reviewed fourteen plays by H. A. Jones and did five drawings of him. The drawing reproduced here may have been inspired by the London performance of Jones's *The Hypocrites,* which he reviewed on 7 September 1907 (*LT,* pp. 313-16). The miniature American flag in Jones's hand probably refers to the success the play had previously had in the United States. Beerbohm owned copies of five of the dramatist's books, all inscribed to him by the author (SC 132).

See plate 33.

Mr. Henry Arthur Jones, England's Scourge [1907]
A Book of Caricatures (1907)
HD 834

20

21 Between 1880 and 1910 Henry Arthur Jones and Sir Arthur Wing Pinero (1855-1934) were the twin pillars of the new play writing in England. Pinero, the entertainer of the privileged class, took himself very seriously, and more than any author of his time he sought praise for his work. However, at the zenith of his career "his themes were becoming repetitious and he had little new to say" (Dunkel, p. 80). His best plays are *The Second Mrs. Tanqueray, The Thunderbolt,* and *Mid-Channel.* The element of "repetitiousness" is wittily brought out in Max's caricature, in which the dramatist's figure, all eyebrows and fur coat, is repeated to infinity in a series of mirrors.

The most notable feature in Pinero's outward appearance was his eyebrows, which jutted in long tufts straight out from his bald, egg-shaped head. Max once observed that these eyebrows were like "the skins of some small mammal, don't you know—just not large enough to be used as mats" (Behrman, p. 170).

Beerbohm was severely critical of Pinero because he was not a "personal force" and stood for no "ideas": "Besides the utter disproportion between his intellectual personality and his constructive skill the main fault to be found with Pinero was his dull and heavy literary style, to which Max variously refers as 'long-winded journalese,' 'fearsome old locutions' and 'ghastly modes of speech,' and which he parodied in 'Mr. Pinero's Literary Style'" [*AT,* pp. 286-90], published 24 October 1903, the year in which this drawing was probably made (Riewald 1953, p. 156).

Max did as many as thirty drawings of Pinero (HD 1161-77, and passim). The drawing reproduced here is an early record of his changing vision of the dramatist (Felstiner 1973, p. 115; see also Felstiner 1972, p. 79 and Fig. 9). It is owned by the Garrick Club, London, which was founded in 1831 as a club in which "actors and men of education and refinement might meet on equal terms." In 1899 Pinero was elected to the General Committee of this Club.

Beerbohm wrote extensive reviews of eleven of Pinero's plays (see *AT, MT,* and *LT,* passim). He owned a presentation copy of Pinero's *The Thunderbolt* (SC 174).

See plate 64.

Mr. Arthur Wing Pinero [1903]
Courtesy of the Garrick Club, London
HD 1164

21

22

According to Beerbohm, George Bernard Shaw (1856-1950) "was a better man than Harris; but Max did not like him much either. His first meeting with him had been in 1894 when Max was in London during an Oxford vacation. Shaw had heard him praised as a cartoonist. Suddenly he arrived at the Beerbohms' house on a bicycle: he had ridden many miles to ask Max to do a likeness of himself. Max was less gratified by this than might have been expected. He realized that he was as yet an amateur in his art and suspected that Shaw was actuated less by admiration than by a desire for the publicity the cartoon might bring him. Max also found Shaw's appearance unappetizing; his pallid pitted skin and red hair like seaweed. And he was repelled by the back of his neck. 'The back of his neck was especially bleak; very long, untenanted, and dead white,' he explained" (Cecil, p. 166).

Max's caricature represents G.B.S. as devil, his scaly tail wound over one arm, and flames rising round him. It is not dated, but *A Book of Caricatures,* in which it occurs, was published in November 1907. The drawing may have been made on the occasion of the performance of the dream-interlude "Don Juan in Hell" from Shaw's *Man and Superman* by Vedrenne-Barker at the Court Theatre, London, on 4 June 1907. The play (apart from the hell scene) had been first produced under the auspices of the Stage Society at the Court Theatre on 21 May 1905. It was directed by Granville Barker, who also took the part of the hero, John Tanner, who was made up like a youthful edition of the author, with a red beard and Mephistophelean eyebrows. The hell scene occurs in the third act. In this scene John Tanner has a dream in which he becomes Don Juan, while Mendoza, the chief of the brigands in whose hands he finds himself, becomes the Devil. In reviewing this performance Beerbohm praised the agility of Shaw's brain, the spontaneity of his humor, and the certainty of his wit (*LT*, p. 297).

Beerbohm owned several of Shaw's books, some of them inscribed to him by the author (SC 200-05).

See plates 23-27, 33.

Mr. Bernard Shaw [1907]
A Book of Caricatures (1907)
HD 1486

22

23 The drawing shows the bearded playwright standing on his head, quizzically observed by Max on one of his infrequent visits to England. After his marriage in 1910, Beerbohm retreated to Rapallo, in the Italian Riviera, where he lived, except during the two wars, until his death in 1956. He was in London for a month or two in the winter of 1912, and again early in 1913, to arrange for an exhibition of his caricatures at the Leicester Galleries to be held in the spring.

Like most Shaw caricatures by Max, the drawing displays the dramatist "in sloppy dress, which for Beerbohm meant that he was inartistic" (Felstiner 1973, p. 85). It was probably inspired by the following lines from *Alice's Adventures in Wonderland:*

> "You are old, Father William," the young man said,
> "And your hair has become very white;
> And yet you incessantly stand on your head—
> Do you think, at your age, it is right?", *etc.*
>
> Lewis Carroll, *The Complete Works,* p. 56.

It would seem that writers on literature have sometimes been (unconsciously) influenced by Max's caricatures. In his *Critical History of English Literature* Professor David Daiches writes: "A favorite device of his [i.e., Shaw's] was to stand the popular view on its head, thus both outraging and titillating his audience" (II, p. 1105). The phrasing of this statement may have been indebted to Max's drawing.

Beerbohm parodied Shaw's thought and style in "A Straight Talk," a preface to an imaginary Shavian Christmas play called *Snt George* (*CG*, pp. 139-47); his "Epitaph for G. B. Shaw" was first published in *MV*, p. 124.

See plates 22, 24-27, 33, 51.

Mr. Bernard Shaw. 1913
Fifty Caricatures (1913)
HD 1499

23

Mild surprise of one who, revisiting England after long absence, finds that the dear fellow has not moved.

24 In this drawing Beerbohm "wittily summed up the way Shaw's genuine comic originality surmounted Ibsen's influence: the 'old clothes' that Shaw was 'selling' for the price of 'immortality' were certainly the threadbare secondhand garments of Ibsen and others, but the brilliant 'patches' were Shaw's own" (Huss, p. 98).

Cf. the following passage from Beerbohm's parody of a Shaw preface: "Flatly, I stole this play. . . . You don't suppose Shakespeare was so vacant in the upper storey that there was nothing for it but to rummage through cinquecento romances, Townley Mysteries, and suchlike insanitary rubbishheaps, in order that he might fish out enough scraps for his artistic fangs to fasten on. Depend on it, there were plenty of decent original notions seething behind yon marble brow. Why didn't our William use *them*? He was too lazy. And so am I" (*CG*, p. 141).

Georg Morris Cohen Brandes (1842-1927), the Danish literary critic and defender of Ibsen, is referred to as a *(mar)chand d'idées* (a dealer in ideas) because he had assimilated the best of contemporary European thought and culture.

In the early nineties Shaw was for some time under the influence of Henrik Ibsen (1828-1906). In 1890 he read a paper on the Norwegian dramatist to members of the Fabian Society, which, in 1891, he expanded into *The Quintessence of Ibsenism.*

For the German philosopher Arthur Schopenhauer (1788-1860) the "real" was not the rational, but the irrational; the metaphysical will is "blind," an insatiable force without conscious purpose or direction. One of Shaw's leading ideas was that a man should consciously live as an "instrument of a Will or Life Force that uses him for purposes wider than his own" (*Major Barbara*). According to Friedrich Nietzsche (1844-1900) the higher state for which man strives is the overman (*Übermensch*). Shaw's "Superman" consciously carries out the purposes of the Life Force.

Beerbohm had reviewed the English translation of Brandes's *Ibsen and Björnson* (*MT*, pp. 173-77); he had also "wrestled with Schopenhauer for a day or so, in vain" (*AEN*, p. 291).

See plates 22, 23, 25-27, 33.

Life-Force, Woman-Set-Free, Superman, etc. 1914
A Survey (1921)
HD 1500

24

Georg Brandes ('Chand d'Idées): "What'll you take for the lot?"
George Bernard Shaw: "Immortality."
Georg Brandes: "Come, I've handled these goods before! Coat, Mr. Schopenhauer's; waistcoat, Mr. Ibsen's; Mr. Nietzsche's trousers—"
George Bernard Shaw: "Ah, but look at the patches!"

25 The initials A. B. W. refer to Arthur Bingham Walkley (1855-1926), drama critic of *The Times.* His article in *The Times* is entitled "Superbity. The Preface to 'Saint Joan.' Mr. Shaw and M. France." [i.e., Anatole France, the French writer].

Max's drawing shows "an enormous white-bearded Shaw propped up over a wispy, artsy-craftsy crowd of incense-burning devotees. Shaw is ecstatically breathing in the fumes" (Buckley, p. 100). The gentleman on the left—a caricature of A. B. Walkley—comments: "And calls himself a non-smoker!"

Another caricature of Shaw by Max (HD 1485) has the caption: "Magnetic, he has the power to infect almost everyone with the delight that he takes in himself."

On 14 April 1914 Beerbohm wrote to his friend Reggie Turner: "I saw . . . the waxen effigy of G.B.S. when I was in London. . . . Some days later I was lunching at his place, and mentioned the effigy to him; at which he flushed slightly, and waved his hands, and said he had *had* to give Tussaud a sitting, as 'it would have seemed so *snobbish* to refuse'! Considering that it had been the proudest day in his life, I was rather touched by this account of the matter. I am afraid he is afraid of me" (*LRT,* p. 230). In February 1921 he wrote in his copy of Sir William Rothenstein's *Twenty-Five Portraits:* "[Shaw] has prostituted his wit, certainly; and made a drudge of her too. But she can stand it. She's gigantic!" (SC 183).

See plates 22-24, 26, 27, 33.

Courtesy of the Humanities Research Center, the University of Texas at Austin

HD 1509

25

"Mr. Shaw's apotheosis is one of the wonders of the age".
—A.B.W. in *The Times,* July 9, 1924. 1924

26

This caricature, showing the sage of 1924 confronting the vigorous young self of the 1890s, is one of a series of drawings entitled "The Old and the Young Self," first exhibited at the Leicester Galleries, 17 April-16 May 1925, and subsequently published in *Observations.* In this series "nineteen persons now in late life are confronted by themselves in youth, so that they see the difference between what they are and what in those days they expected to become. The series, which contains some of Max's favourite subjects, Gosse, Kipling, Shaw, Bennett, etc., is the best thing in the volume. Max is on his home ground dealing with individuals not abstractions, and with an extraordinary penetration. No wonder that he did not envy the young. Why should he, when advancing years were so full of interest to the observer of the human comedy? Who would have though that the bohemian young Rothenstein would grow into such a pillar of respectability and the serious Asquith into a *bon viveur*; that Lloyd George should have changed so much and George Moore so little!" (Cecil, p. 409).

Max did no less than forty-three caricatures of Shaw (not counting those in which the dramatist occurs without being the principal figure), and reviewed no less than twenty or so of his plays and books. This means that there are more caricatures of Shaw than of anyone, except Max himself and King Edward VII, and that of all living playwrights Shaw had the largest number of articles devoted to him by Beerbohm—Arthur Wing Pinero being a good second. Yet, in spite of this prolonged critical attention, Max could never make up his mind about what he called the "most salient phenomenon 'around theatres'" in his day. When writing the Epistle Dedicatory to *Around Theatres* in 1924, his "lamentable" vicissitudes in the matter of G.B.S. still amused him very much. These "vicissitudes" chiefly arose from his lasting doubts about Shaw's ability to create living human characters (Riewald 1953, pp. 158, 160).

See plates 22-25, 27, 33.

The Old and the Young Self: Mr. Bernard Shaw. 1924
Observations (1925)
HD 1510

26

Old Self: "Strange! You strike me as frivolous, irreligious, and pert; full of a ludicrous faith in mankind and in the efficacy of political propaganda; squalidly needy in circumstances, and abominably ill-dressed. . . . And I used to think you quite perfect!"

27 The drawing is an "improved" full-page photograph of Shaw as the Socialist, and "the change in the Socialist's appearance is startling, even diabolical. He coruscates with lurid color: his teeth are incandescent; his green billycock hat sports a feather; below his chin are a vast dotted ascot, a pear-shaped pearl; and his eyes gleam like Dracula's" (Behrman, p. 27).

The drawing faces p. 116 of Beerbohm's copy of Archibald Henderson's *George Bernard Shaw, his Life and Works: A Critical Biography* (London: Hurst and Blackett, 1911), extensively annotated and the plates altered by the artist. "Henderson's book was a work of naïve hero-worship: a hero-worship unshared by Max, and not evident in Henderson's book after Max had finished with it. With the aid of an erasing knife, Indian ink and colour wash, he worked at it for more than a year, interpolating passages into the text, superimposing grotesque features or costumes on the various persons portrayed in the illustrations, Morris, Sidney Webb and, of course, Shaw himself. In one picture Max has transformed the youthful Shaw into a Mephistophelean figure with a diabolical smile and wearing a green bowler hat with a feather" (Cecil, p. 374).

The following passage is from Beerbohm's comment in the form of a "Note to Prof. Henderson," written round the plate: "In the Spring of '91 Eleanor Marx had given to him [*scil.* Shaw], as a token of esteem, a green billycock hat which had belonged to her father in his *bourgeois* days. 'It went,' says Shaw, 'to my head.' He feverishly applied himself to the task of dressing 'up to' it. Having succeeded in doing this, he offered himself as a candidate for admission to the Marlborough House Set, but, owing to the influence of Baron Hirsch (who could not, or would not, forget that the hat had belonged to Karl Marx), he was rejected. In deep bitterness of spirit he fell back on the Tivoli Bar, where he perceptibly coarsened. This was a very sad time for all Shaw's friends." The Marlborough House Set was the "fast" set led by the Prince of Wales who lived at Marlborough House, London. Maurice de Hirsch, Baron Hirsch auf Gereuth (1831-96), the German-born capitalist and

The Socialist [n. d.]

Courtesy of the Henry W. and Albert A. Berg Collection, the New York Public Library, Astor, Lenox, and Tilden Foundations

not in HD

27

THE SOCIALIST.

From a photograph taken in July, 1891.

philanthropist, was the founder of the Jewish Colonization Association. 27

The half-title of the book is inscribed: "For W[illiam]. A[rcher]. with affectionate regards from Max. Rapallo, June 1920." Underneath, in imitation of Henderson's hand, he has written: "and from me too—Archibald Henderson. North Carolina." When Archer died, he stipulated in his will that the volume should be returned to Beerbohm; it is now in the Berg Collection of the New York Public Library.

Archibald Henderson, of the University of North Carolina, is the author of several books on Shaw. The original photograph of Shaw was taken in July 1891.

See plates 22-26, 33.

28 Sir James Matthew Barrie (1860-1937), the Scottish dramatist and novelist, "represents another aspect of the anti-naturalistic tendency which made itself felt in *fin-de-siècle* drama and literature. With him, as with Shaw and Wilde, the reaction took the form of a flight into the fantastic comedy. But in each writer the accent was differently placed. In Shaw it was on the intellectual and funny fantastic, in Wilde on the witty fantastic, and in Barrie on the humorous and sentimental fantastic. Of the three modes Max loved that of Wilde best. Next came Barrie's method, and finally that of Shaw—though on one occasion he professed that he preferred Shaw to Barrie. Yet this isolated assertion is not borne out by the actual trend of his criticisms. It is true, Barrie could do with a little more logic; and it might be doubted whether children, who are not naturally sentimental, could be really amused by *Peter Pan*. But for the rest his praise is superlative. *Quality Street* was 'sweetly pretty'; *The Admirable Crichton*, which might almost be ranked with *The Importance of Being Earnest*, was 'the most delightful achievement of the past few years,' 'quite the best thing' that had happened, in his time, to the British stage; the Gilbertian *Peter Pan* was the artistic medium through which he expressed the child in him, 'the child, as it were, in its bath, splashing, and crowing as it splashes'; it was 'the best thing' he had done, 'the most directly from within himself,' and its excellence was only topped by *Alice Sit-by-the-Fire*. Lastly, the fantastic method of *What Every Woman Knows* was far more truly (if only symbolically) related to life than the realistic method of the average dramatist" (Riewald 1953, p. 162).

All the same, "there was something in Barrie's personality that antagonized [Beerbohm]. Though not averse to the sentimental if it was administered discreetly and with a grain of irony to save it from sickliness, Max found Barrie's brand altogether too lush and sticky. Further, he doubted if it expressed a genuine emotion" (Cecil, p. 261).

The drawing represents "the little man . . . always so shy & retiring" (Rothenstein to Beerbohm, 3 November 1929, *MW*, p. 132) holding an enormous pipe which stands on the floor and emits clouds of smoke. Barrie smoked a large pipe all his life. The pieces collected in his last book of articles, *My Lady Nicotine* (1890), are supposed to be written by a seasoned smoker. Reviewing a performance of Barrie's *Old Friends* on

Mr. J. M. Barrie. 1912
Courtesy of the Ashmolean Museum, Oxford
HD 102

28

12 March 1910, Beerbohm wrote: " . . . having read *Ghosts*, [Mr. Barrie] 28
lit his pipe, and, in the fumes, wove a little theory of heredity on his own account" (*LT*, p. 535).

In May 1912 Barrie presented a statue of Peter Pan, the work of Sir George Frampton, to Kensington Gardens; this may have been the immediate occasion for Beerbohm's drawing.

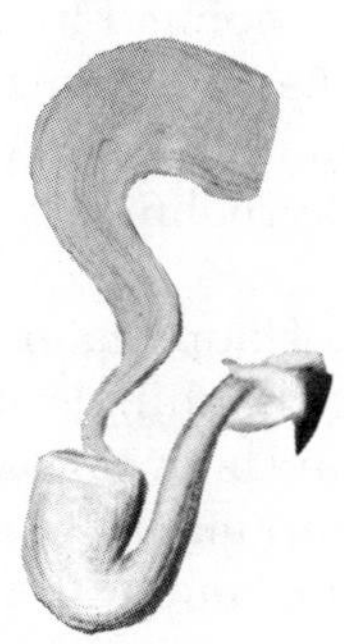

29 Gerhart Hauptmann (1862-1946), the German playwright, novelist, and poet, had a house in Rapallo in the Riviera di Levante, where the Beerbohms lived. It was William Rothenstein who, on a visit to Rapallo in 1926, introduced Max and Florence to the Hauptmanns; and though Max spoke no German and Gerhart no English, they soon became friends, each recognizing the other's genius through the interpretative skill of Florence. In August 1926 Rothenstein wrote Beerbohm that he had received a letter from the Hauptmanns in which Gerhart referred to Max in these words [*translation*]: "You have put us in touch with the Beerbohms, and for that my very special thanks. He also belongs among the gold grains that remain in the sieve. If Rapallo attracts me, then Beerbohm with his evenness of temper, his philosophy and his exemplary mode of life has become a decisive factor. The hours in his house, with the four of us sitting at his round table, remain in Grete's and my memory with deep significance" (*MW*, p. 126, n. 3).

The second Lady Beerbohm, Elisabeth Jungmann (1897-1959), had been for many years Gerhart Hauptmann's secretary. After the death of Lady Florence Beerbohm in 1951, Miss Jungmann became Beerbohm's assistant and secretary. Beerbohm married her a month before his death in 1956.

The drawing shows Hauptmann, "Goethe in plus fours, doing a metronomic walk along the shingle at Rapallo, his handsome, noble face uplifted to let the wind blow through his hair" (Behrman, p. 208; it has been shown that Hauptmann's works were influenced by Goethe). When Thomas Mann, the famous German novelist, came to Rapallo, he used to call Hauptmann " 'The President of the Republic of Letters.' That's how Hauptmann was regarded, and that is how he regarded himself" (loc. cit.).

Beerbohm reviewed two of Hauptmann's plays, *The Thieves' Comedy* and *Lonely Lives* (*AT*, pp. 365-69; *MT*, pp. 364-65). He also wrote an (unpublished) essay in memory of him (SC 381).

On the drawing Hauptmann's first name is spelled "Gerhardt."

Fifty Caricatures (1913)
HD 728

29

Gerhart Hauptmann, making the most of the Riviera di Levante. 1912

30 Beerbohm admired Maurice Maeterlinck (1862-1949), the Belgian playwright and poet, author of *Pelléas et Mélisande* (1892), as a great poet and a fascinating thinker, and especially praised his dramatic power. His "shadowy enigmatic little dramas moved him deeply because he felt Maeterlinck's view of life so true" (Cecil, p. 176). The Belgian dramatist was, in fact, "one of the greatest of living writers," and certainly "the most loveable writer of his age" (*MT*, p. 479). Reviewing *Pelleas and Melisande* on 25 June 1898, Beerbohm praised the "enchantment," the "delicate and vague spell" of Maeterlinck's "marvellous and lovely play" (ibid., pp. 38, 39).

Jacques-Émile Blanche (1861-1942), the French portrait painter and writer, was nicknamed "the French Sargent" on account of his popularity with Edwardian society people. His portraits include those of Charles Conder, Aubrey Beardsley, Arthur Symons, Walter Sickert, George Moore, Henry James, Max Beerbohm, and Thomas Hardy. Some of these are in the Tate Gallery, London; the portrait of Beerbohm is in the Ashmolean Museum, Oxford (see *The Times*, 1 November 1947, p. 8). Blanche's *Portraits of a Lifetime: The Late Victorian Era, The Edwardian Pageant, 1870-1914* (London: J. M. Dent, 1937, and New York: Coward-McCann, 1938) and *More Portraits of a Lifetime, 1918-1938* (London: J. M. Dent, 1939) contain references to Max Beerbohm.

Blanche once referred to Maeterlinck as a "boor." But many years later the two became friends and Blanche painted the portrait of Maeterlinck, now in the Rouen Museum.

The word "eagerly" does not appear on the drawing.

Courtesy of the Art Institute of Chicago
HD 146

30

M. Jacques Blanche eagerly combating M. Maurice Maeterlinck's reluctance to be painted [1907]

31 The title of this drawing, *Celtades Ambo* (both of them Celts), was inspired by *Arcades Ambo* (both of them denizens of Arcady) in Virgil's *Eclogue VII*, 4. The two "Celts" are the Irish dramatist Edward Martyn (1859-1924) and William Butler Yeats (1865-1939). Yeats is standing on the right; as usual, he is caricatured "lanky and wavering, with thin hands and a shock of dark hair" (Felstiner 1973, p. 116). The drawing was first published in *The Daily Chronicle* (London), 26 May 1899.

In 1893 Yeats had published a collection of stories under the title *The Celtic Twilight: Men and Women, Ghouls and Faeries.* His verse play, *The Countess Cathleen,* was first performed in Dublin in 1899. This event, together with the performance of Edward Martyn's play *The Heather Field,* marked the foundation of the Irish Literary Theatre. Max's drawing was inspired by the Dublin performance of these two plays, which he attended in his capacity as dramatic critic for the *Saturday Review.* Though Yeats was not a dramatist in the sense in which Maeterlinck was one, Beerbohm thought *The Countess Cathleen* "a poem of exquisite and moving beauty," while *The Heather Field* impressed him as "a very powerful play indeed" (*MT*, pp. 143, 144).

Beerbohm once wrote Florence that "though Yeats was a genius, geniuses were usually asses, and Yeats's particular asininity bored him" (Mix, p. 140). He expressed himself even more strongly in his alternative ending to Yeats's "The Ballad of the Foxhunter," written in his copy of the first edition of Yeats's *Poems* (1899), and beginning:

> Hark forard, away, and down with Yeats!
> Begorra, he droives me mad.

He also owned an "improved" copy of H. S. Krans's study, *William Butler Yeats and the Irish Literary Revival* (1904) (SC 138, 249).

See plates 32, 51, 64.

Celtades Ambo [1899]
Courtesy of the Robert H. Taylor Collection, Princeton, N. J.
HD 1825

31

32 Here the poet and dramatist is seen "seriously presenting the mildly bewildered novelist, who is sucking the knob of his cane, to the Queen of the Fairies" (Lynch, p. 128).

The movement for the foundation of an Irish theater and for a national Irish renaissance was warmly supported by George Moore (1852-1933), the author of naturalistic novels and himself an Irishman.

From an essay written by Beerbohm in 1914 it appears that he was bothered by Yeats's preoccupation with symbolism, the occult, and Celtic lyricism: "Ireland, so far from being more rarefied, is grosser than she appears in my atlas. There may be in that land fairies and phantoms, and whispering reeds, and eternal twilight, and wan waters, and tears leading blind men . . . From time immemorial Ireland has been harbouring human beings. Poetry that hasn't the human note can no more be truly Celtic than it can be truly Saxon or Mongolian or Slav. . . . the pleasure of meeting Yeats was not for me an unmixed one. I felt always rather uncomfortable, as though I had submitted myself to a mesmerist who somehow didn't mesmerise me" ("First Meetings with W. B. Yeats," *MA*, pp. 96-97).

The conceit of "tears leading blind men" also occurs in Beerbohm's parody of Yeats's early style, printed in the same volume, pp. 95-96:

> From the lone hills where Fergus strays
> Down the long vales of Coonahan
> Comes a white wind through the unquiet ways,
> And a tear shall lead the blind man.

The (partly imaginary) titles of the books on the shelf are: *Realism: Its Cause & Cure; Half Hours with the Symbols; Life of Kathleen Mavourneen; Erse without Tears; Songs of Innocence; Murray's Guide to Ireland; Short Cuts to Mysticism.* In 1892 Yeats had compiled a collection of *Irish Fairy Tales,* illustrated by his brother.

See plates 31, 32, 33, 51, 64, 88-91.

32

Mr. W. B. Yeats, presenting Mr. George Moore to the Queen of the Fairies [1904]

33 The person taking the patient's pulse is Harley Granville-Barker (1877-1946), producer and author of "intellectual" plays, and afterwards critic of the theater; see *MV*, pp. 114-17, and SC 97.

The small figures in the background surrounding the "invalid" are from left to right:

St. John Greer Ervine (1883-1971), playwright and novelist; dramatic critic of *The Observer* from 1919 to 1923 and from 1925 to 1939;

Arnold Bennett (1867-1931), novelist and author of successful plays; he helped to make the Lyric Theatre, Hammersmith, prosperous and fashionable;

Thomas Evelyn Scott-Ellis, eighth Baron Howard de Walden (1880-1946), writer and patron of the arts;

George Bernard Shaw (1856-1950);

Henry Arthur Jones (1851-1929), author of realistic plays;

Arthur Bingham Walkley (1855-1926), dramatic critic of *The Times*;

Edward Gordon Craig (1872-1966), actor, producer, and stage-designer; he founded and edited *The Mask*, a journal devoted to the art of the theatre; see SC 46-50;

William Archer (1856-1924), dramatic critic and translator of the plays of Ibsen;

George Moore (1852-1933), the novelist and playwright; Beerbohm knew that Moore liked to boast of his real or imagined love affairs; see plate 90;

John Masefield (1878-1967), Poet Laureate and novelist; he also wrote a number of poetic dramas, which show the influence of the Greek tragic writers.

The text on the drawing reads "complicated by" instead of "complicated with," and "Let's give her" instead of "Let her have."

See further plates 16, 19, 20, 22-27, 51, 88-91, 96-98.

The British Drama (that eternal invalid). 1923.

Courtesy of the William Andrews Clark Memorial Library, University of California, Los Angeles

HD 95

Dr. Granville-Barker: "And how are we to-day? Yes, yes. . . . The old complaint. Cerebral anaemia. And complicated with acute cinematitis. . . . Municipal pillules are the only hope."—Mr. St. John Ervine: "Let her have a strong tonic every Sunday morning."—Mr. Arnold Bennett: "Hammersmith air's all *she* needs."—Lord Howard de Walden: "Get some very rich man to endow her."—Mr. Bernard Shaw: "Try Shavian cathartics!"—Mr. Henry Arthur Jones: "Inject red corpuscles!"—Mr. A. B. Walkley: "Tue la!"—Mr. Gordon Craig: "Give her a Mask!"—Mr. William Archer: "I don't think there's much wrong with her!"—Mr. Masefield: "I think Craig might save her."—Mr. George Moore: "I was once her lover."

34 The drawing represents Sir Noel Coward (1899-1973), the English playwright, composer, theater producer, film director, actor, and author of revues, sketches, lyrics, and short stories. Among his most popular plays were *Easy Virtue* (1925), *Hay Fever* (1925), *Private Lives* (1930), *Cavalcade* (1931), *Design for Living* (1932), and *Blithe Spirit* (1941). In his *Bitter Sweet,* a musical in three acts, originally produced by Charles B. Cochran at His Majesty's Theatre, London, on 18 July 1929, he succeeded in recapturing a mood of "seminostalgic" sentiment.

Heroes and Heroines of Bitter Sweet, Beerbohm's last collection of caricatures, is a portfolio containing five "sentimental" drawings in color of the author, producer, and members of the cast of *Bitter Sweet.* In his prefatory note to this collection, Max writes: "Sentiment is out of fashion. Yet 'Bitter Sweet,' which is nothing if not sentimental, has not been a dead failure. Thus we see that things that are out of fashion do not cease to exist. Sentiment goes on, unaffrighted by the roarings of the young lions and lionesses of Bloomsbury. 'Bitter Sweet' goes on too; and Mr. Cochran (being a sentimentalist) has wished that this survival should be commemorated by me in some sentimental drawings, which are here submitted to you."

Max's drawing of Coward is not a caricature, but a pleasant likeness, done with sympathy. It seems to sum up what a critic, more than twenty years later, saw as the essence of Coward's genius: "One blinks at the garish neon lights, the dizzy succession of plays, the indefatigable energy and the thousand-and-one details seen and remembered by a camera-like mind" (Greacen, pp. 16-17; see also Lesley, passim).

Mr. Noel Coward [*c.* 1931]

Courtesy of the Lilly Library, Indiana University, Bloomington, Indiana

HD 373

34

Part Three

Essayists

---

35. Logan Pearsall Smith, J. C. Squire, and Edward Shanks
36. E. V. Lucas
37. Hilaire Belloc and G. K. Chesterton
38. Belloc at the Vatican
39. G. K. Chesterton
40. The Old and the Young Self: G. K. Chesterton

35 Lloyd Logan Pearsall Smith (1865-1946), the American essayist, critic, and poet, was the author of *Trivia* (1902; literally: *trifles*) and *More Trivia* (1922). According to the *Dictionary of National Biography*, "a certain spiritual timidity . . . almost always prevented him from pursuing subjects of depth or solemnity."

Pearsall Smith had been at Oxford with Beerbohm, and their friendship was long lasting. In his essay "Sir Max Beerbohm," published in the *Atlantic Monthly* (November 1942, pp. 88-90), Smith paid tribute to "his old friend and fellow perfectionist."

Sir John Collings Squire (1884-1958), journalist, playwright, critic, and poet, was literary editor of *The London Mercury* from 1919 to 1934, in which he wrote under the name of "Solomon Eagle." His *Books in General: Second Series* (London: Martin Secker, and New York: Alfred A. Knopf, 1920) contains an essay on Beerbohm's *The Happy Hypocrite,* entitled "Mr. Max Beerbohm's Idyll" (pp. 262-68).

Edward Richard Buxton Shanks (1892-1953), poet, novelist, and critic, was assistant-editor of *The London Mercury* from 1919 to 1922. He reviewed the two volumes of Beerbohm's *Around Theatres* in *Outlook* (London), 29 November 1924, p. 385.

The drawing shows Smith submitting the manuscript, which is the size of a postage stamp, to Mr. Squire. Mr. Shanks stands looking on. Before Smith had seen this caricature, Edmund Gosse warned him at a dinner party: "Logan . . . I feel it is my duty to tell you that something has happened to you that sooner or later happens to us almost all. Max has got you. We don't like it and you won't like it, but you must pretend that you do. You can console yourself at any rate with the thought that it will give uncommon pleasure to your friends" (Mix, p. 150).

Beerbohm owned presentation copies of Smith's *How Little Logan Was Brought to Jesus* (1934) and *Afterthoughts* (1931), both with inscriptions by the author, and of Shanks's *The Island of Youth* (1921) (SC 208, 99).

See plate 64.

A Survey (1921)

HD 1556

From left to right: Edward Shanks, J. C. Squire, Logan Pearsall Smith.

35

The author of "Trivia" submitting his latest MS. to the conductors of "The London Mercury". 1921

36

Edward Verrall Lucas (1868-1938), journalist, essayist, and critic, was the editor of *The Works of Charles and Mary Lamb* (7 vols., 1903-05) and *The Letters of Charles Lamb, to which are added those of his sister Mary* (3 vols., 1935), and the author of *The Life of Charles Lamb* (2 vols., 1905). He also wrote about thirty collections of light conversational essays, but these are sometimes marred by sentiment. Lucas was for many years a contributor to *Punch. The Book of the Queen's Dolls' House Library,* edited by Lucas (London: Methuen, 1924), contains a facsimile reproduction of Beerbohm's contribution entitled "Meditations of a Refugee." Lucas's *Post-Bag Diversions* (London: Methuen, 1934) contains parts of three letters written to him by Max Beerbohm.

When Bohun Lynch asked Beerbohm's assistance for his book *Max Beerbohm in Perspective* (1921), Beerbohm suggested to the prospective author to compare him as essayist with other essayists, and to point out, among other things, "how much lighter E. V. Lucas' touch is than mine" (Lynch, p. ix). Of course Beerbohm's advice was double-edged.

A week after the death of E. V. Lucas, Beerbohm published a short tribute to him in the *Sunday Times* ("A Memorable Companion," 3 July 1938).

Mr. E. V. Lucas. 1923
Things New and Old (1923)
HD 981

36

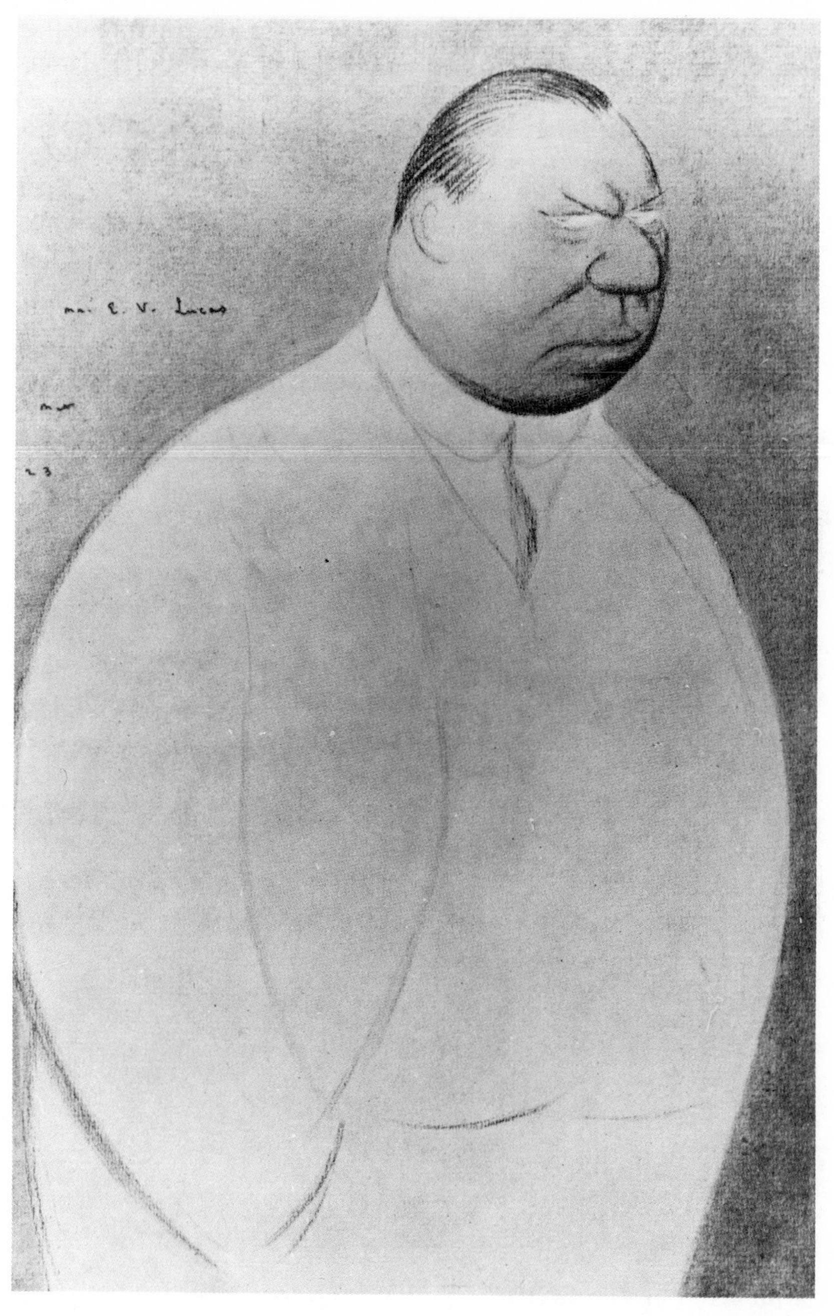

37 The drawing shows "a gesticulating Belloc standing on a chair to lecture the gross, overfed Chesterton on religious doctrine" (McElderry 1972, p. 136).

Joseph Hilaire Pierre Belloc (1870-1953), the French-born English historian, poet, and essayist, was a Roman Catholic. Gilbert Keith Chesterton (1874-1936), the English essayist, poet, novelist, and critic, was an Anglican by baptism, but was received into the Roman Catholic Church in July 1922. Geneva, the city of John Calvin's theocracy, stands for Protestantism.

"Two complex men Max greatly admired as writers and liked as friends were G. K. Chesterton and Hilaire Belloc. 'They had blind spots,' he said, 'but they were delightful men. Such enormous gusto, you know, such gaiety, and feeling for life.'. . . Max told me he felt that Belloc was, on occasion, a victim of monomania. 'He had the conviction that there was only a single lane to Heaven'" (Behrman, pp. 280-82). Max teased Belloc alternately with paying him compliments. " 'When you really get talking, Hilary, ' he once said to him, 'you are like a great Bellocking ram, of like a Roman river full of baskets and dead cats.' . . . 'Of course . . . I can only speak for man; but Mr. Belloc knows God's point of view'" (Cecil, pp. 262, 406).

Beerbohm parodied Belloc's thought and style in "Of Christmas" (*CG*, pp. 131-37). See also Beerbohm's poem "In the Store-Room at King's Land," *MV*, p. 124, and plates 38, 39, 40.

A Book of Caricatures (1907)
HD 121

37

Mr. Hilaire Belloc, striving to win Mr. Gilbert Chesterton over from the errors of Geneva. 1907

38 Though the drawing is dated 1920, Hilaire Belloc did not visit the Pope in that year. It was during his mission to the Vatican in the summer of 1916 that he was received in private audience by Pope Benedict XV. In 1920, the year in which the drawing was made, Belloc published his *Europe and the Faith,* a book which created a sensation. Its theme is the Catholic conscience of history, i.e., only the Catholic "sees Europe from within." On 16 May 1920 he wrote to his friend J. S. Phillimore that "there [was] not the least chance yet of England's conversion," but that the Faith had to be *presented* by the English Catholics. Of course Belloc was thinking of a mass conversion to Roman Catholicism. T. S. Eliot, writing in 1931, was certainly not the only person with a different opinion: "If England is ever to be in any appreciable degree converted to Christianity, it can only be through the Church of England" ("Thoughts after Lambeth," *Selected Essays 1917-1932,* p. 359).

Beerbohm thought highly of Belloc's poems. In a letter to his friend Reggie Turner, written 10 April 1926, he referred to them as "very certainly classic" (*LRT,* p. 261). His parody "After Hilaire Belloc," inspired by such Belloc poems as "Noël" and "Heretics All" (*CG,* p. 136; rpt. in *MV,* pp. 34-35), is a good-natured criticism of the lyrical quality of Belloc's songs, of his mastery of cadence, his medievalizing Catholicism, and his admiration of French poetry.

Max's library contained a copy of the 1916 edition of Belloc's *The Path to Rome,* which had been presented and inscribed to him by the author. He also owned copies of Belloc's *First and Last* (1912), *Sonnets and Verse* (1923), *The Cruise of the "Nona"* (1925), *Belinda* (1928), and *In Praise of Wine* (1933), most of them with autograph presentation inscriptions from the author to Max Beerbohm (SC 31-35).

The caption on the drawing is in French.

See plate 37.

Mr. Belloc's Visit to the Vatican. 1920
A Survey (1921)
HD 122

38

THE POPE: "They tell me, my son, that you are a prophet."
MR. BELLOC: "I am, Your Holiness. And also I have a talent for drawing very pretty diagrams. Here is one of them, showing that in England the national conversion will take place some time between May and July, 1923."

39 The drawing represents Chesterton making an after-dinner speech, the curve of his belly going on almost endlessly, and his shirt showing under his waistcoat. "Chesterton's huge stomach stands partly for [his] love of food, partly for another quality . . . his faith in his own girth as the measure of things" (Felstiner 1973, p. 158).

Max was amused by Chesterton, when he first met him in 1902. "'Enormous apparition,' he noted down. 'Head big for body—way of sinking head on chest. Like a mountain and a volcanic one—constant streams of talk flowing down—paradoxes flung up into the air—very magnificent'" (Cecil, p. 200).

Chesterton had taken Beerbohm as part model for Auberon Quin, the humorist hero of his romance *The Napoleon of Notting Hill,* illustrated by W. Graham Robertson, and published by John Lane in 1904. The pictures of Auberon Quin are all in the likeness of Max, but the character itself is much more like Chesterton than Beerbohm. Max was pleased at the way he had been identified with King Auberon. "All right, my dear chap," he said to Chesterton, who was trying to apologize. "Mr. Lane and I settled it all at lunch" (Cecil, p. 201).

Beerbohm parodied Chesterton's thought and style in "Some Damnable Errors about Christmas" (*CG*, pp. 45-52).

See plates 37 and 40.

G. K. Chesterton [1912]
Courtesy of the Ashmolean Museum, Oxford
HD 312

39

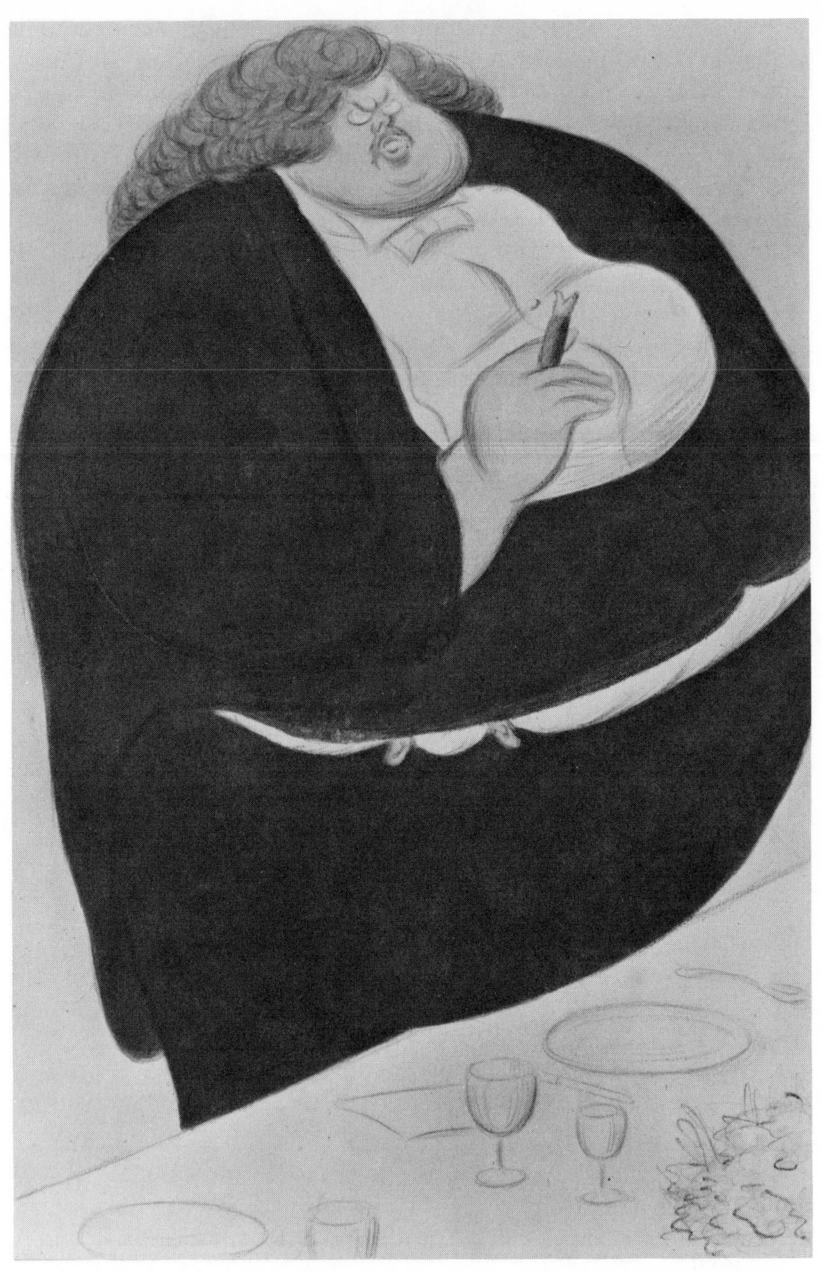

40

One of a series of drawings entitled "The Old and the Young Self," but not included in *Observations* (1925); see plate 26.

Chesterton was twenty-six when he first met Hilaire Belloc, and was strongly influenced by him, especially as far as his political, sociological, and historical views were concerned. The phrases of Chesterton's Young Self recapitulate some of the key concepts which Belloc, at one time or another, handled in his publications.

Beerbohm did not think much of Chesterton's work. The essays in *What's Wrong with the World?* (1910) he thought "very cheap and *sloppy*, though with gleams—gleams of gas-lamps in Fleet Street mud and slush," and he believed that Chesterton's writings did not wear well at all (*LRT*, 15 November 1910 and 15 February 1911, pp. 193, 194). "I am not nearly so witty as Chesterton for one," Max once wrote. "But certainly I have not prostituted and cheapened my wit as he has" (Cecil, p. 370).

The Autobiography of G. K. Chesterton (New York: Sheed & Ward, 1936) contains a note on Max Beerbohm on pp. 94-95. Maisie Ward's *Gilbert Keith Chesterton* (London: Sheed & Ward, 1944) has a four-line poem by Chesterton on Beerbohm (p. 135).

See plates 37 and 39.

The Old and the Young Self: Mr. G. K. Chesterton. 1925
Courtesy of the Ashmolean Museum, Oxford
HD 314

40

YOUNG SELF: "Oh yes, I drank some beer only the other day, and rather liked it; and of course the Crusades were glorious. But all this about English public life being honeycombed with corruption, and about the infallibility of the Pope, and the sacramental qualities of beer, and the soul-cleansing powers of Burgundy, and the immaculate conception of France, and the determination of the Jews to enslave us, and the instant need that we should get straight back into the Middles Ages, and"—

OLD SELF: "Well, you haven't met Belloc."

Part Four

Rossetti and His Circle

---

41. Rossetti's Courtship
42. John Ruskin meets Miss Cornforth
43. Coventry Patmore at Spring Cottage
44. The Small Hours in the 'Sixties at 16, Cheyne Walk
45. Gabriel and Christina
46. George Meredith's Hortation
47. Swinburne and Edmund Gosse
48. Theodore Watts-Dunton, F. J. Shields, and Hall Caine
49. Dante Gabriel Rossetti, in his back garden
50. At the Pines

41

Dante Gabriel Rossetti (1828-82), the English painter and poet, was one of the original members of the Pre-Raphaelite Brotherhood, formed in 1848. The other members were William Holman Hunt, John Everett Millais, Rossetti's brother William Michael Rossetti, Frederic George Stephens, James Collinson, and Thomas Woolner, the sculptor. Agreeing that British painting of their own day required drastic reformation, they resolved to paint, not according to rules, like the imitators of Raphael, but according to nature. Apart from individual differences, their pictures have in common "a definiteness of contour, an avoidance of *chiaroscuro,* and a deliberately novel use of color, applied on a luminous ground," and, more importantly, "an overmastering concern for proliferated, minute detail" (Lang, pp. xi-xii). Their work is further characterized by its medievalism, introspection, and symbolism, by "the famous image of a woman with large, staring eyes and masses of heavy hair" (Hunt, pp. xi-xii), and by its religious and instructive quality (Grieve, p. 24).

It was in 1850 that Rossetti fell in love with a beautiful red-haired girl, a milliner's assistant named Elizabeth Siddal, who was to become the favorite model of the Pre-Raphaelite Brotherhood. They became engaged in a year or so. In November 1852 Rossetti left home to live at 14 Chatham Place, London. Eight years later "Lizzie" became his wife. There is no proof that Elizabeth Siddal was Rossetti's mistress before he married her; that she became pregnant soon after their marriage suggests that she had kept him at a distance.

Max's drawing of Elizabeth Siddal is a masterly synthesis of Rossetti's portraits of her (cf. Surtees, plates 421-29, and passim for Elizabeth Siddal as model). William Michael Rossetti described his brother's wife as a "most beautiful creature . . . tall, finely formed, with a lofty neck, and regular somewhat uncommon features, greenish-blue unsparkling eyes, large perfect eyelids, brilliant complexion, and a lavish heavy wealth of coppery-golden hair" (Lang, p. xvii).

"While one who knows nothing about Rossetti would expect a display of passion in a drawing with that caption, and a person who knows something about him would anticipate a show of affection, at the least, the drawing shows the poet and Elizabeth Siddal standing several feet apart, very bored, contemplating space. A mouse sits quietly

Rossetti's Courtship. Chatham Place, 1850-1860. 1916
Courtesy of the Tate Gallery, London
HD 1270

41

on the floor. Both the contrast between what one would ordinarily expect of lovers and what we know of this love affair, and an exaggeration of the passivity of Rossetti's ardor are brought out by this drawing" (Stevenson, pp. 144-45).

Elizabeth Siddal continually appears in Rossetti's paintings and poems. Gabriel's infatuation with "Lizzie" is the subject of Christina Rossetti's sonnet

In an Artist's Studio

One face looks out from all his canvases,
One selfsame figure sits or walks or leans:
We found her hidden just behind those screens,
That mirror gave back all her loveliness.
A queen in opal or in ruby dress,
A nameless girl in freshest summer-greens,
A saint, an angel—every canvas means
The same one meaning, neither more nor less.
He feeds upon her face by day and night,
And she with true kind eyes looks back on him,
Fair as the moon and joyful as the light:
Not wan with waiting, not with sorrow dim;
Not as she is, but was when hope shone bright;
Not as she is, but as she fills his dream.

24 December 1856.

The Poetical Works of Christina Georgina Rossetti, p. 330.

See plates 42-46, 48, 49, 55, 60.

42 Dante Gabriel Rossetti and Elizabeth Siddal were an ill-matched couple, and their married life was strained and unhappy. Elizabeth's health declined, and in 1862 she died from an overdose of laudanum. Overwhelmed by remorse, Rossetti thrust into her coffin his manuscript poems, which were subsequently disinterred and published.

In 1856 or 1857 another woman, Fanny Cornforth (whose real name was Sarah Cox), had entered Rossetti's life. She was a "low-born, ill-bred, illiterate, voluptuous and gorgeous" girl (Lang, p. xvii), and, in the early sixties, became Rossetti's model, mistress, and non-resident "housekeeper."

Of the ladies—that is, the models employed by the members of the P.R.B.—Max preferred "the healthy Fanny Cornforth to the doomed Elizabeth Siddal. It must have been hard work for the Pre-Raphaelites to be constantly ethereal, and Miss Cornforth was bosomy and earthy. She afforded the Pre-Raphaelites a nice change from Pre-Raphaelitism; she was Rubensy" (Behrman, p. 276).

In 1866 John Ruskin (1809-1900), the English art critic and social reformer, published a little book entitled *The Ethics of the Dust: Ten Lectures to Little Housewives on the Elements of Crystallisation* (London: Smith, Elder & Co.). These lectures had been given, in substance, as the author states in his preface, at a girls' school in the country. They were a mixture of mineralogy, theology, economics, moral homilies, and Egyptian mythology. Beerbohm's imagination must have been tickled by the contrast between Ruskin's dryasdust intellectualism and the more "fleshly" values of the elephantine Fanny Cornforth; he must have known that Ruskin's marriage had been annulled on the grounds of impotence. It must be added that Ruskin's relationship with Rossetti was founded on loyalty and admiration.

The figure in the center of the drawing is Dante Gabriel Rossetti. The picture of Fanny Cornforth is an evocation of his portraits of her (cf. Surtees, plates 399, 400, and passim for Fanny as model). Ruskin's head conforms to the following description of it in a contemporary critique of the lectures which he delivered in 1853: "Mr. Ruskin has light sand-coloured hair; his face is more red than pale; the mouth well cut, with a good deal of decision in its curve, though somewhat wanting

An Introduction. 1916

Courtesy of the Tate Gallery, London

HD 1272

42

MISS CORNFORTH: "Oh, very pleased to meet Mr. Ruskin, I'm sure."

in sustained dignity and strength; an aquiline nose; his forehead by no means broad or massive, but the brows full and well bound together" (Cook, I, p. 321). On the back wall is a painting of the unhappy Elizabeth Siddal. 42

From Beerbohm's letter to Reginald Turner, written 8 October 1906, we know that he had read Ruskin's *The Stones of Venice* (1851-53) "with much deiight and surprised reverence for Ruskin" (*LRT*, p. 170).

See plates 41, 43-46, 48, 49, 55, 60.

43

The second half of the nineteenth century was characterized by a hectic cult of beauty. It was the Pre-Raphaelite painters who, by their careful and thorough methods, were among the first to turn the public's attention to the beauty of design and color of household utensils. Thus artists like D. G. Rossetti, Ford Madox Brown, and William Holman Hunt themselves designed and painted furniture, but it was William Morris who brought about a complete revolution in the artistic taste of the British public.

For a few years the English poet Coventry Patmore (1823-96) was closely associated with the Pre-Raphaelites, but his interest was purely personal, and he afterwards disclaimed all conscious relationship to their artistic creed.

The woman in the drawing is Rossetti's wife, Elizabeth Siddal. After their marriage in 1860 the Rossettis took rooms at Spring Cottage, Downshire Hill, Hampstead, London.

Coventry Patmore's long poem *The Angel in the House* (1854-56) is a celebration of married love and happy domestic life. It was inspired by his first marriage. The following lines are from "The Epilogue" to this poem:

> Ah, dearest Wife, a fresh-lit fire
> Sends forth to heaven great shows of fume,
> And watchers, far away, admire;
> But when the flames their power assume,
> The more they burn the less they show,
> The clouds no longer smirch the sky,
> And then the flames intensest glow
> When far-off watchers think they die.

The Poems of Coventry Patmore, p. 205.

See plates 41-42, 44-46, 48, 49, 55, 60.

Spring Cottage, Hampstead, 1860. 1917
Courtesy of the Tate Gallery, London
HD 1279

43

Coventry Patmore comes round from Elm Cottage yonder, and very vehemently preaches to the Rossettis that a tea-pot is not worshipful for its form and colour, but rather as one of the sublime symbols of Domesticity.

44 In the summer after Elizabeth Siddal's ambiguous death in 1862, Rossetti leased a quaint old house, with an immense garden and magnificent paneled rooms, in Cheyne Walk, Chelsea, London, to be shared with brother William Michael, Algernon Charles Swinburne, and George Meredith. But the bachelor *ménage* soon broke up as a result of their temperamental differences.

Algernon Charles Swinburne, the English poet, lived from 1837 to 1909. His "Anactoria," a savage, Sapphic poem, was published in *Poems and Ballads* (1866), the first collection of his lyrics. It was begun in an attempt to render Sappho's so-called "Ode to Anactoria," chiefly with the idea to analyze a type of forbidden passion:

> I would find grievous ways to have thee slain,
> Intense device, and superflux of pain;
> Vex thee with amorous agonies, and shake
> Life at thy lips, and leave it there to ache;
> Strain out thy soul with pangs too soft to kill,
> Intolerable interludes, and infinite ill;
> Relapse and reluctation of the breath,
> Dumb tunes and shuddering semitones of death.

From "Anactoria," *Poems and Ballads,* p. 66.

The drawing shows Swinburne reading to the two brothers from 'Anactoria.' "William is sitting dead somber; the widower Gabriel slumps on a chaise longue, scowling painfully" (Felstiner 1973, p. 75).

Beerbohm, like many others of his generation, was fascinated by Swinburne, "the flammiforous boy of the dim past—a legendary creature, sole kin to the phoenix" (*AEN*, p. 58). But with all his love of the man, Max had never been blind to his faults as a poet. Though he admired his "sheer joyous power of song" (ibid., p. 59), he objected to the overwhelming exuberance of his rhapsodies, which stun the ordinary reader before impressing him (*M*, p. 95).

See plates 41-43, 45-50, 55, 60.

The Small Hours in the 'Sixties at 16, Cheyne Walk.—Algernon reading "Anactoria" to Gabriel and William. 1916

Courtesy of the Tate Gallery, London

HD 1275

44

45 The drawing shows Rossetti and his austere sister "as they are examining a selection of brightly-coloured Liberty silks" (Rothenstein, p. 12). "Beerbohm must have envisaged this scene as taking place a few months before Gabriel's death, at a time when the young Edmund Gosse found the aging Christina a decidedly formidable and unattractive personage, and complained that her subfusc appearance was particularly 'hard to bear from the high priestess of Pre-Raphaelitism.' During later life she grew even plainer and quieter, gradually retreating into an 'impenetrable reserve.' 'Her gloomy religion,' wrote a niece, 'was not far removed from pessimism.' She was 'a short, stout, elderly woman,' remembered another, 'with dark prominent eyes and heavy laden complexion,' almost always 'dowdily dressed in black'" (Quennell).

In his question, Rossetti is referring to the opening lines of Christina's poem "A Birthday," dated November 18, 1857:

My heart is like a singing bird
Whose nest is in a watered shoot:
My heart is like an apple-tree
Whose boughs are bent with thickset fruit;
My heart is like a rainbow shell
That paddles in a halcyon sea;
My heart is gladder than all these
Because my love is come to me.

Raise me a dais of silk and down;
Hang it with vair and purple dyes;
Carve it in doves and pomegranates,
And peacocks with a hundred eyes;
Work it in gold and silver grapes,
In leaves and silver fleurs-de-lys;
Because the birthday of my life
Is come, my love is come to me.

The Poetical Works of Christina Georgina Rossetti, p. 335.

Courtesy of the Tate Gallery, London
HD 1278

ROSSETTI, HAVING JUST HAD A FRESH CONSIGNMENT OF "STUNNING" FABRICS FROM THAT NEW SHOP IN REGENT STREET, TRIES HARD TO PREVAIL ON HIS YOUNGER SISTER TO ACCEPT AT ANY RATE ONE OF THESE AND HAVE A DRESS MADE OF IT FROM DESIGNS TO BE FURNISHED BY HIMSELF. 1917

D. G. R. "What *is* the use, Christina, of having a heart like a singing bird and a water-shoot and all the rest of it, if you insist on getting yourself up like a pew-opener?"

C. R. "Well, Gabriel, I don't know—I'm sure you yourself always dress very quietly."

In all matters of taste D. G. Rossetti's influence has been immense. 45
The purely decorative arts he may be said to have rejuvenated directly or indirectly. Inspired by him, William Morris (1834-96), the poet, designer, typographer, and socialist thinker, succeeded in winning back his countrymen to the richness and frank color of formal floral and heraldic pattern in silk textiles and to the gaiety and freshness of vegetable dyes, as distinct from the crude colors produced by the aniline dyes then commonly used.

On the drawing itself the last sentence of the legend reads: "C. R. (mildly) "'Well, Gabriel, I don't know. I'm sure you yourself always dress very simply.'"

See plates 41-44, 46, 48, 49, 55, 60

46 George Meredith (1828-1909), the English novelist and poet. Dante Gabriel Rossetti was one of his intimate friends. Beerbohm especially admired Meredith's earlier manner:

"It must be twenty-five years since I had read [*The Adventures of Harry Richmond*], and I had only the haziest memory of them; and I feared they might be less golden than the haze made them appear to me. And oh, lo! how much *more* golden they were than I had remembered. *What* a book! *What* swiftness and beauty and strength! It is the flight of a young golden eagle high across seas and mountains—beholding which, one likens H[enry]. J[ames]. to a very old mole burrowing very far down under a very poky back-garden in South Kensington. I mean, one likens the author of the *A*[*wkward*]. *A*[*ge*]. to that mole. I won't hear a word against the rest of H[enry]. J[ames]'s later manner. But I will willingly hear any number of words against G[eorge]. M[eredith]'s own later manner. For I turned from *Harry Richmond* to *Diana of the Crossways,* a book which had also become dim to me. And oh, the difference!—oh the tedious, crack-jaw, arid intellectual snobbery of *Diana*! . . . *Diana* is as dead as a door-nail, and I tremble to think what *The Amazing Marriage* and *Lord Ormont* must be as dead as!" (*LRT*, p. 249; letter dated 18 May 1920).

Meredith's *The Adventures of Harry Richmond* was published in 1871; *Diana of the Crossways* in 1885; *Lord Ormont and his Aminta* in 1894; and *The Amazing Marriage* in 1895. Henry James's *The Awkward Age* appeared in 1899.

Hendon is in northwest London; from Cheyne Walk, Chelsea, to Hendon is about eight miles. In the right-hand bottom corner of the drawing Max has written "Autumn 1862."

Beerbohm parodied Meredith's thought and style in "The Victory of Aphasia Gibberish" (*The Saturday Review,* Christmas Supplement, 1896). An improved version of this, entitled "Euphemia Clashthought," was published in *CG,* pp. 167-76. On 12 March 1910 Beerbohm reviewed the London performance of Meredith's *The Sentimentalists* (*LT,* pp. 533-36). See also *MV*, p. 56, and plates 41-45, 48, 49, 55, 60.

Courtesy of the Tate Gallery, London
HD 1274

46

Rossetti insistently exhorted by George Meredith to come forth into the glorious sun and wind for a walk to Hendon and beyond. 1916

47 Edmund William Gosse (1849-1928), the English critic and poet, formed many literary friendships. He became a specially close friend of Algernon Charles Swinburne (1837-1909), of R. L. Stevenson (1850-94), and of Henry James (1843-1916). He wrote an excellent but somehow incomplete *Life* of Swinburne (1917), and edited his *Letters* (2 vols., 1918, with Thomas James Wise) and his *Complete Works* (The Bonchurch Edition, 20 vols., 1925-27, also with Wise).

From 1862 Dante Gabriel Rossetti lived at 16 Cheyne Walk, Chelsea, near the river. The drawing shows Gosse and Swinburne walking on the Embankment, on their way to Rossetti. "The tiny Swinburne, his flying red hair crowned by a topper, is followed by the bespectacled Gosse, book in hand. What will the quietly studious Gosse make of the moody, flamboyant Rossetti?" (McElderry 1972, pp. 142-43). Swinburne's "bewitching childishness . . . is . . . engagingly caught in the caricature of the poet drawing Mr. Gosse by the hand to see Rossetti. We can see in it . . . the very movement of a child, the irresponsibility, the straining eagerness to hurry" (Lynch, p. 97).

See plates 41-46, 48-50, 55, 60, 63, 64.

Courtesy of the Tate Gallery, London
HD 1643

47

Riverside Scene. Algernon Swinburne taking his great new friend Gosse to see Gabriel Rossetti. 1916

48 Theodore Watts-Dunton (1832-1914), the poet, novelist, critic, and solicitor, and Hall Caine (1853-1931), the novelist, were Rossetti's acolytes at 16 Cheyne Walk in his last, declining years. It was they who, having largely invented the absurdly romantic Rossetti legend in Rossetti's lifetime, vigorously propagated it after his death (Rossetti, *Letters,* I, p. xix).

In this drawing Watts-Dunton is admonishing Caine, who knows that he "carries greatness in each hand, in the shape of two manuscripts of his own, which he is determined to read to Rossetti. He is, plainly, not going to take the advice that Watts-Dunton is offering him. Frederic Shields . . . is standing near Watts-Dunton, backing him up. In the background, lying-sitting on a sofa, is Rossetti, corpulent, brooding, hearing the argument that concerns him but not listening" (Behrman, p. 277).

Hall Caine's *Recollections of Dante Gabriel Rossetti* appeared in 1882. He then retired and wrote a number of tremendously popular novels, many of them centered in the Isle of Man. In 1912 Beerbohm remembered him as follows: "I had written, in more than one of the public prints, very irreverently, very gallingly about some of [his] works. My caricatures of that worker . . . they too had appeared in the public prints. With all the ribaldry of youth, I had persecuted Hall Caine" ("Nat Goodwin—and Another," *MA*, p. 65; broadcast 30 May 1949).

Frederic James Shields (1833-1911), the English painter and decorative artist, was influenced by the Pre-Raphaelite paintings which he saw at the great Manchester Exhibition of 1857, and afterwards became one of Rossetti's close friends.

Among the curiosities Rossetti liked to collect were Japanese screens and "Blue," i.e., the Chinese porcelain of the seventeenth and eighteenth centuries (Gaunt 1945, p. 39).

The legend on the drawing has the words "this evening" instead of "to-night." The caption, "Quis Custodiet Ipsum Custodem?" (Who will guard the guard himself?) is an adaptation of Juvenal's "Sed quis custodiet ipsos custodes?" (*Satirae*, VI, 347-48).

See plates 41-46, 49, 50, 55, 60, 84.

Quis Custodiet Ipsum Custodem? 1916
Courtesy of the Tate Gallery, London
HD 1277

THEODORE WATTS: "Mr. Caine, a word with you! Shields and I have been talking matters over, and we are agreed that to-night and henceforth you *must* not and *shall* not read any more of your literary efforts to our friend. They are too—what shall I say?—too luridly arresting, and are the allies of insomnia."

49 An early caricature of the Rossetti circle, showing Dante Gabriel Rossetti, with his friends, in his back garden. In the background, from left to right: Algernon Charles Swinburne (1837-1909), the poet; Theodore Watts-Dunton (1832-1914), the critic and novelist; George Meredith (1828-1909), the novelist and poet; Hall Caine (1853-1931), the novelist. In front of the wall on the left is James Abbott McNeill Whistler (1834-1903), the American painter and etcher, whose white forelock is being pulled by Swinburne; Watts-Dunton's finger is held up in staid admonition. The figure with the kangaroo is Edward Coley Burne-Jones (1833-98), the painter and designer. The person standing upright and reciting is William Morris (1834-96), the poet, artist, and socialist. On the right one sees William Holman Hunt (1827-1910), the Pre-Raphaelite painter, and in front of him, in profile, John Ruskin (1819-1900), the writer on art, economics, and sociology. In the foreground is Rossetti himself. The red-haired model is no one in particular; just a vague synthesis, though she looks more like Fanny the Sumptuous (as her friends used to call her) than like poor neurotic Lizzie (cf. Rossetti's portraits of Fanny Cornforth, Surtees, plates 399, 400, and passim for Fanny as model).

One of Rossetti's recreations was the collecting of curiosities, including strange animals. During the sixties he possessed "kangaroos, a wallaby, a chameleon, some salamanders, wombats, an armadillo, a marmot, a woodchuck, a deer, a jackass, a racoon and smaller animals galore. The birds included peacocks, parakeets, Chinese horned owls and a raven. . . . He bought a Brahmin bull" (Gaunt 1942, pp. 114-15).

See plates 41-48, 50, 52, 53, 55, 60, 84.

Dante Gabriel Rossetti, in his back garden [1904]
The Poets' Corner (1904)
HD 1268

49

50 This lovely drawing shows Algernon Charles Swinburne (*left*), and Theodore Watts-Dunton (*right*). The painting on the wall represents the dark-haired Jane Burden, a beautiful Oxford girl, who had sat to William Morris as a model and who had become his wife in 1859; she seems to be gazing down at the old men with an air of incredulity (cf. Rossetti's portraits of her, Surtees, plates 407-09, and passim for Jane as model).

In 1879 Watts-Dunton removed his friend Swinburne to his house No. 2, The Pines, at the foot of Putney Hill, in southwest London, when the poet appeared to be dying of delirium tremens. Watts-Dunton became his officially appointed guardian and, for thirty years, exercised a devoted and tactful control over him, making him live a life entirely at variance with the sort of life implied by his poetry.

Beerbohm first called on Swinburne and Watts-Dunton in 1899. When in 1914 Edmund Gosse asked him to contribute a little pen-portrait of Swinburne to his forthcoming biography of the poet, Max wrote his charming reminiscential essay "No. 2. The Pines," included in *And Even Now*.

[No. 2. The Pines:] "No. 2—prosaic inscription! But as that front-door closed behind me I had the instant sense of having slipped away from the harsh light of the ordinary and contemporary into the dimness of an odd, august past. Here, in this dark hall, the past was present. Here loomed vivid and vital on the walls those women of Rossetti whom I had known but as shades. Familiar to me in small reproductions by photogravure, here they *themselves* were, life-sized, 'with curled-up lips and amorous hair' done in the original warm crayon, all of them intently looking down on me while I took off my overcoat—all wondering who was this intruder from posterity" (*AEN*, pp. 61-62).

[Watts-Dunton:] "... the dear little old man ... something gnome-like about his swarthiness and chubbiness ... the shaggy hair that fell over the collar of his eternally crumpled frock-coat, the shaggy eyebrows that overhung his bright little brown eyes, the shaggy moustache that hid his small round chin ... very cosy and hirsute, and rather like the dormouse at that long tea-table which Alice found in Wonderland" (ibid., pp. 63, 72-73).

[Swinburne:] "Watts-Dunton sat at the head of the table, with a

At the Pines [n. d.]
Courtesy of the Ashmolean Museum, Oxford
HD 1647

50

huge and very Tupperesque joint of roast mutton in front of him, 50
Swinburne and myself close up to him on either side. He talked only to me. This was the more tantalising because Swinburne seemed as though he were bubbling over with all sorts of notions. Not that he looked at either of us. He smiled only to himself, and to his plateful of meat, and to the small bottle of Bass's pale ale that stood before him—ultimate allowance of one who had erst clashed cymbals in Naxos. This small bottle he eyed often and with enthusiasm, seeming to waver between the rapture of broaching it now and the grandeur of having it to look forward to" (ibid., p. 65).

See Panter-Downes, and also plates 44, 47-49.

Part Five

Aesthetes and Decadents

---

51 From left to right, *back row:* Richard Le Gallienne (1886-1947), the poet and essayist; Walter Richard Sickert (1860-1942), the impressionist painter; George Moore (1852-1933), the novelist and playwright; John Davidson (1857-1909), the poet; Oscar Wilde (1854-1900); William Butler Yeats (1865-1939); and (just showing) perhaps "Enoch Soames."

Front row: Arthur Symons (1865-1945), the poet and critic; Henry Harland (1861-1905), the novelist; Charles Conder (1868-1909), the artist; William Rothenstein(1872-1945), Principal of the Royal College of Art, London; Max Beerbohm (1872-1956); Aubrey Beardsley (1872-98), the illustrator. With the exception of the American-born Henry Harland, the persons in the drawing are all English or Irish.

The books referred to are Holbrook Jackson, *The Eighteen Nineties: A Review of Art and Ideas at the Close of the Nineteenth Century* (London: Grant Richards, 1913; Pelican Books, 1939), and Osbert Burdett, *The Beardsley Period: An Essay in Perspective* (London: John Lane, 1925). Holbrook Jackson's book is dedicated to Max Beerbohm and has a chapter on him entitled "The Incomparable Max."

The most brilliant satire on the Aesthetes and Decadents of the Nineties is Beerbohm's story "Enoch Soames" (*SM*, pp. 3-48).

See plates 23, 31-33, 54-58, 64, 66, 89-91.

Courtesy of the Ashmolean Museum, Oxford
HD 1650

51

Some Persons of "the Nineties" little imagining, despite their Proper Pride and Ornamental Aspect, how much they will interest Mr. Holbrook Jackson and Mr. Osbert Burdett. 1925

52 James Abbott McNeill Whistler (1834-1903), the American painter, settled in Chelsea, London, in 1863, but in his later years he lived mainly in Paris. He was the most important link between English and French aestheticism. Among his best-known pictures are the "Portrait of the Artist's Mother, " which is now in the Luxembourg, Paris, and the Thames "Nocturnes." In 1878 he brought a libel action against Ruskin for denouncing one of his nocturnes, and was awarded a farthing damages. Whistler's *The Gentle Art of Making Enemies,* published in 1890, contains his pungent comments on criticisms of his works.

Beerbohm's favorable review of the second edition of *The Gentle Art of Making Enemies* ("Papillon Rangé," *The Saturday Review,* 20 November 1897, pp. 546-47) occasioned Whistler to congratulate the editor of *The Saturday Review* on his latest acquisition—"your new gentleman—a simple youth, of German extraction—'belockter Jüngling' " (ibid., 27 November 1897, p. 592), though he took exception to some of Beerbohm's remarks.

In his essay entitled "Whistler's Writing," written a year after the painter's death, Beerbohm observes of Whistler: "He was inordinately vain and cantankerous. Enemies . . . were a necessity to his nature; . . . Quarrelling and picking quarrels, he went his way through life blithely. . . . Whistler's insults always stuck—stuck and spread round the insulted, who found themselves at length encased in them, like flies in amber" (*YA*, pp. 106, 116).

The following impression of Whistler is from Beerbohm's notebook: "Tiny—Noah's Ark—flat-brimmed hat—band almost to top—coat just not touching ground—button of the Legion of Honour—black gloves—Cuban belle—magnificent eyes—exquisite hands, long and lithe—short palms" (Cecil, p. 157).

Whistler's hair was both thick and black. His one single white lock of hair, which he said was inherited, appeared fairly early in life and became a sort of flag. He called it his "white feather." His silk hat was, in Beerbohm's words, "a real *nocturne*" (*W*, p. 19).

See plates 49 and 53.

Mr. Whistler [n. d.]

Courtesy of the Houghton Library, Harvard University

HD 1773

52

53 It was James Whistler who, in the sixties and seventies, started the craze for Chinese blue and white painted porcelain in England.

The drawing shows Whistler, "a wee young man with a mop of black ringlets and a quizzing glass" (Beerbohm's words: Mix, p. 28), his white lock of hair protruding, in his studio, enthusing on the beauty of a large blue porcelain Nankin vase to his neighbor in Chelsea, the essayist and historian Thomas Carlyle (1795-1881), author of *Sartor Resartus* (1833-34), a philisophy of clothes. The "Sage of Chelsea", towering and dyspeptic, looks on in dismal unbelief. Of course the gospel of "Art for Art's sake" preached by Whistler was entirely foreign to Victorian England. The caricature, as Lynch remarks, suggests to us that "the art of making enemies, though gentle, was quite easy" (p. 149).

One of Whistler's most notable portraits is the "Portrait of Thomas Carlyle," painted in 1872, and now in the Glasgow Civic Collection. Carlyle was persuaded to give sittings after he had inspected and admired the portrait of the artist's mother.

Carlyle's clothes seem to illustrate Beerbohm's remark in "Dandies and Dandies": "That any one who dressed so very badly as did Thomas Carlyle should have tried to construct a philosophy of clothes, has always seemed to me one of the most pathetic things in literature." For Max, Carlyle's battered hat, that is still preserved in Chelsea, formed an important clue to *Sartor Resartus*, "that empty book" (*W*, p. 8).

See plates 49 and 52.

Blue China. 1916
Courtesy of the Tate Gallery, London
HD 241

53

54 This impression of Oscar Wilde (1854-1900), the Anglo-Irish dramatist, poet, novelist, and essayist, was first published in *Pick-Me-Up* (London), 22 September 1894, a year before Wilde's trials at the Old Bailey. The drawing was used as evidence against him after he had been arrested. In 1911 Max wrote that it "showed only the worse side of [Wilde's] nature. At the time when I did [it], and even when it was published, I hardly realised what a cruel thing it was: I only realised that after Oscar's tragedy and downfall" (HD 1783).

Beerbohm's awareness of the penalties exacted by success has always been acute (cf. plate 103). He once said: " . . . as Oscar became more and more successful, he became arrogant. He felt himself omnipotent, and he became gross not in body only . . . but in his relations with people. He brushed people aside; he felt he was beyond the ordinary human courtesies that you owe people even if they are, in your opinion, beneath you" (Behrman, p. 85).

"Wilde he has caricatured many times, without much variation; and Max has made the most of his peculiar hands. The fingers were extremely pointed, the thumb curved sharply back like a claw in reverse. The whole effect in the caricatures of this hand is that of a kind of crab, the elaborately jewelled ring being its eye" (Lynch, p. 119).

Beerbohm's word picture in his private character book gives a more detailed impression: "Luxury—gold-tipped matches—hair curled—Assyrian—wax statue—huge rings—fat white hands—not soigné—feather bed—pointed fingers—ample scarf—Louis Quinze cane—vast malmaison—catlike tread—heavy shoulders—enormous dowager—or schoolboy—way of laughing with hands over mouth—stroking chin—looking up sideways—jollity overdone—But real vitality— . . . Effeminate, but vitality of twenty men. Magnetism—authority—Deeper than repute or wit—Hypnotic" (Cecil, p. 71).

Max owned first editions of Oscar Wilde's *Intentions* (1891), *Salomé: Drame en un Acte* (1893), and *The Ballad of Reading Gaol* (1898); he also had a copy of the 1908 edition of *De Profundis* (SC 240-44).

See plates 51 and 55.

Oscar Wilde [1894].
Courtesy of the Ashmolean Museum, Oxford
HD 1779

54

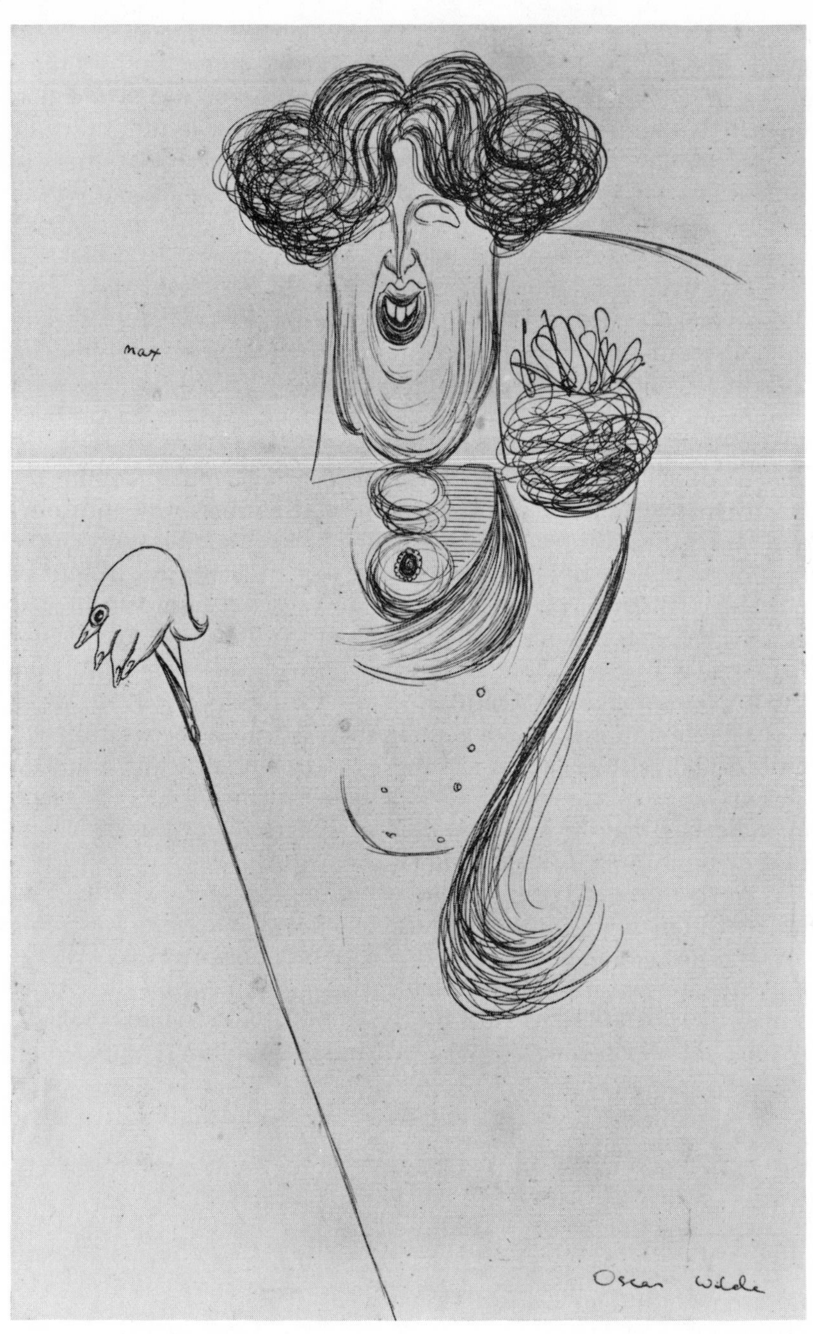

55 From 2 January to 27 December 1882 Oscar Wilde, the leader of the Aesthetic Movement, lectured in the United States on such subjects as "The English Renaissance" and "The Ethics of Art." No known manuscripts of "The House Beautiful," used by Wilde on his lecture tour, survive; however, his tour received coverage in American and Canadian newspapers, and a collation of the accounts of the lecture indicates that he was influenced by Ruskin's and Morris's attempts to bring beauty into the lives of the middle class (O'Brien).

Max's drawing shows the founder of the Aesthetic Movement, dressed in a puce-colored "Aesthetic" costume (i.e., knee-breeches) and holding a calla lily in his hand, confronting an audience consisting of greatly bewildered bearded old farmers. On the wall is a picture of Abraham Lincoln, symbol of the common man, with American flags behind it.

Wilde exhorted his American audiences "to abandon morality for beauty, to liberate art from didactic purpose, to beautify dress, furniture, and pots. He told them of Rossetti, Swinburne, and Whistler. Of the sunflower and the lily he observed: 'We love these flowers in spite of what Mr. Gilbert may tell you, not for any vegetable fashion at all, but because they are elegant in design'" (Tindall, p. 7). Wilde's passion for the lily may be traced back to the symbolism of flowers typical of the Pre-Raphaelite creed of Truth to Nature (Gaunt 1945, p. 105).

The affectations of Aesthetes and Aestheticism had been satirized in Gilbert and Sullivan's musical *Patience,* produced at the Standard Theatre on Broadway in 1881. It made an instantaneous hit, which was an indication that the American public might be interested in a lecture tour by the famous British Aesthete.

Beerbohm rated Wilde disconcertingly high as a serious writer, and he even praised his poetry. "But about his character he was more penetrating and less favourable" (Cecil, p. 124). His principal writings on Wilde are: [anon.] "Oscar Wilde by an American," *Anglo-American Times*, 25 March 1893, rpt. in *LRT*, pp. 285-92; "A Peep into the Past," written in December 1893, or very early in 1894, publ. in *PP*, pp. 3-8; an

Courtesy of the Tate Gallery, London
HD 1784

55

The name of Dante Gabriel Rossetti is heard for the first time in the United States of America. Time: 1882. Lecturer: Mr. Oscar Wilde. 1916

obituary article, as part of "A Satire on Romantic Drama," *The Saturday Review*, 8 December 1900, pp. 719-20, rpt. in *MT*, pp. 333-34; "A Lord of Language" [review of *De Profundis*], *Vanity Fair*, 2 March 1905, p. 309, rpt. in *PP*, 37-40; and, between 1902 and 1909, reviews of several of Wilde's plays, rpt. in *AT*, *MT*, and *LT*. 55

Instead of the words "United States" the caption on the drawing has "Western States."

For Dante Gabriel Rossetti see also plates 41-46, 48, 49, 60; for Oscar Wilde see plates 51 and 54.

56 John Davidson (1857-1909), the Scottish poet and playwright, author of the *Fleet Street Eclogues* (1893, 1896) and of other poems and plays, was "bitterly at odds with the world. It was surprising that he and Max should be friends; for Davidson was an uncompromising and brooding Scot, with a temper exacerbated by poverty and neglect and asserting defiantly a Nietzschean creed of splendid ruthlessness, in a style that blended thundering romantic rhetoric with rough modern colloquialism. As a matter of fact Max found Davidson's poetry hard reading although he admired it: 'His violent buffeting of clouds meant nothing to me,' he relates. 'But,' he goes on, 'he was an authentic man of genius and had all the sweetness of his tribe'" (Cecil, p. 133).

In a letter, dated 30 January 1908, to Grant Richards, his London publisher, John Davidson himself gave a most accurate analysis of Beerbohm's caricature of him in the following words: "It is doubtless one of the cleverest [of Beerbohm's drawings]—a presentation of the terrible intellectual disease, swelled head. The face and skull are entirely disfigured by the turgidity of the brain, of the thyroid gland, and of the pharyngeal organs; the eye crushed out of position; the nose is extended and spread like an inverted snout; the hat has to be carried in the hand as it is much too small for the head; the body becomes stunted; the other extremities small in sympathy with the cranium; and a constant vertigo requires the assistance of a staff to maintain an erect posture" (Townsend, pp. 383-84).

Beerbohm reviewed Davidson's play *Godfrida* (*MT*, pp. 69-72) and his dramatization of Victor Hugo's *Ruy Blas* (*AT*, pp. 308-10). He also wrote a parody of Davidson's style and thought, entitled "I and Matter (Preface to 'Hell: A Harlequinade')" (*The Saturday Review*, 8 December 1906, pp. 703-04), in which he represented his beloved friend as a philosopher-clown stabbing himself. After Davidson's suicide in 1909 Beerbohm did not reprint this parody in *A Christman Garland* (1912).

Max owned a presentation copy of Davidson's *The Testament of John Davidson* (1908), inscribed to him by the author, and also copies of three of Davidson's other books, all first editions, and inscribed to him by the author (SC 53, 54).

See plate 51.

Mr. John Davidson. 1907
A Book of Caricatures (1907)
HD 408

56

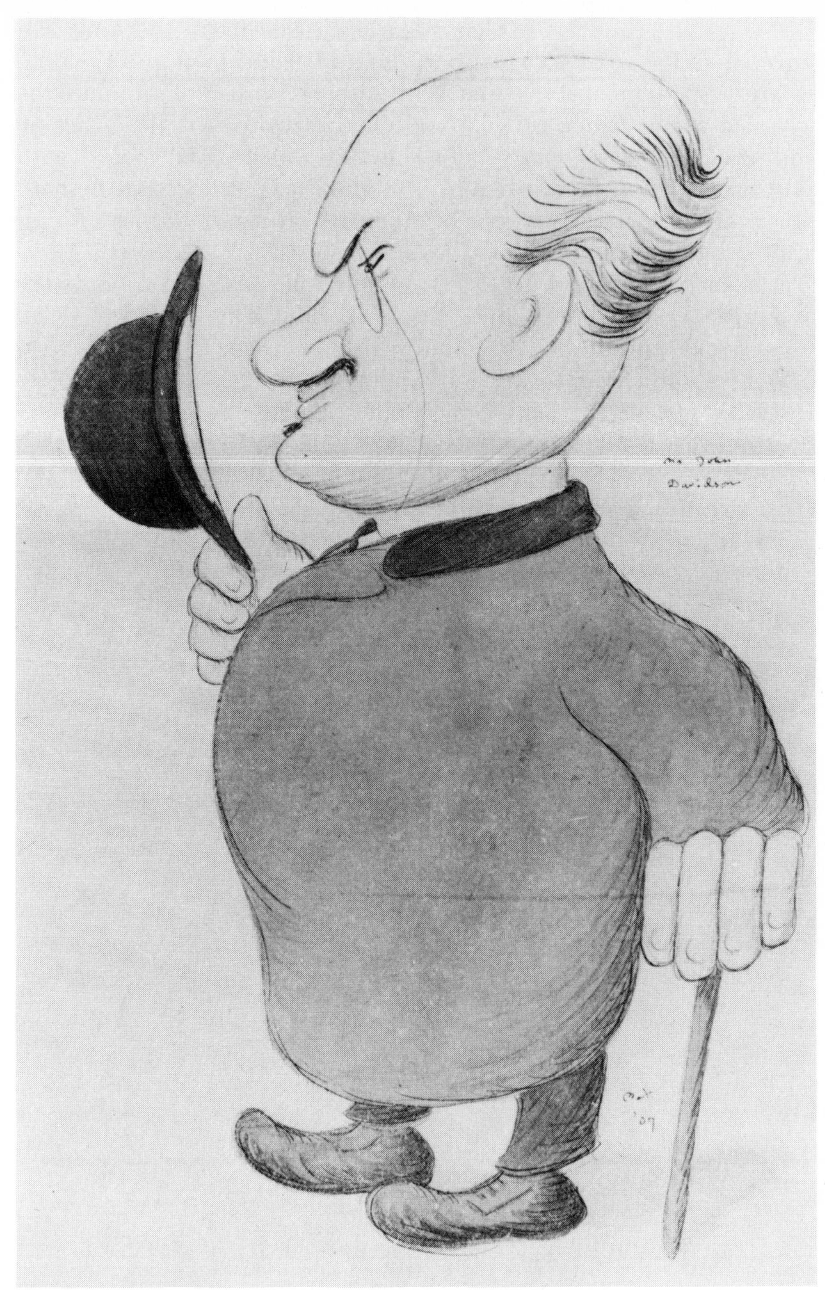

57 Henry Harland (1861-1905), the American novelist and journalist, went to Paris in 1889 and thence to London, where he spent most of his time. With Aubrey Beardsley he founded the *Yellow Book,* which he edited from 1894 to its demise in 1897. "After the ending of the *Yellow Book* . . ., the Harlands watched Max's career with proprietary interest and when in 1898 Max succeeded George Bernard Shaw as dramatic critic of the *Saturday Review,* they read him approvingly" (Mix, p. 23).

In each issue of the *Yellow Book* Harland published a short story and critical essays signed "The Yellow Dwarf." One of these, "Dogs, Cats, Books, and the Average Man" (July 1896, pp. 11-23), deals with Max Beerbohm. Max's caricature of Harland, entitled "The Yellow Dwarf," appeared in the October 1896 issue of this quarterly. Beerbohm's prose contributions to it—"1880," "King George the Fourth," "The Pervasion of Rouge," and "Poor Romeo!"—were included in *The Works of Max Beerbohm* (1896), his first collection of essays.

Harland's work shows the influence of de Maupassant and Henry James. His best-known novel is *The Cardinal's Snuff-Box* (1900).

See plate 51.

Henry Harland Esq [1896]
Caricatures of Twenty-Five Gentlemen (1896)
HD 707

57

Henry Harland Esq

58 Richard Le Gallienne (1866-1947), poet, critic, and belle-lettrist, author of *The Romantic '90s* (1925), had been a contributor to the *Yellow Book*. In 1896, the year in which Max's *Caricatures of Twenty-Five Gentlemen* was published, Le Gallienne's romantic novel *The Quest of the Golden Girl*, which had then just come out, was a popular success (cf. Beerbohm's review of it in the *Daily Mail*, 13 February 1897, p. 4), though it was parodied almost at once. Beerbohm himself parodied Le Gallienne's thought and style in "The Blessedness of Apple-Pie Beds," *The Saturday Review*, Christmas Supplement, 1896. Two years later Le Gallienne moved to New York. In 1902 Max chided him gently on a postcard with the following verse:

To Dick

O witched by American bars!
Pan whistles you home on his pipes.
We love you for loving the stars,
But what *can* you see in the stripes?

MV, p. 16.

In the drawing Le Gallienne, all hair and no face, is represented as a tiny figure strolling among the stars. His "cloudy fuzz of hair hiding his ineffective face expresses Max's view of his cloudy ineffective art" (Cecil, p. 137). Referring to Le Gallienne, Beerbohm once wrote: "Why does the man's very name sound ungrammatical?" (*LRT*, p. 86).

Beerbohm owned presentation copies of Le Gallienne's *Prose Fancies: Second Series*, *Retrospective Reviews*, and *The Quest of the Golden Girl*, all published in 1896, and the first and last of these inscribed to him by the author (SC 140). The caricature probably epitomizes Max's impression of these volumes. He also had in his library a presentation copy, with inscription, of Le Gallienne's *Rudyard Kipling: A Criticism*, with a bibliography by John Lane (1900) (SC 139; see plate 72).

See also plate 51.

Richard Le Gallienne [1896]
Caricatures of Twenty-Five Gentlemen (1896)
HD 912

58

RICHARD · LE · GALLIENNE MAX

Part Six

A Variety of Writers

---

59. In the Shades
60. John Morley brings John Stuart Mill
61. Matthew and Mary Augusta Arnold
62. The Great Biography
63. Austin Dobson and Edmund Gosse
64. The Old and the Young Self: Sir Edmund Gosse
65. The Old and the Young Self: Cunninghame Graham
66. Frank Harris
67. Rudyard Kipling
68. De Arte Poetica
69. Rudyard Kipling composing "The Absent-Minded Beggar"
70. Rudyard Kipling takes a bloomin' day aht
71. The Old and the Young Self: Rudyard Kipling
72. Rudyard Kipling's Soul
73. Logic and Mathematics Reconciled
74. Walter de la Mare
75. Lytton Strachey
76. Echo
77. Osbert and Sacheverell Sitwell

59 "In the Shades—1915" was specially drawn for, and presented by the artist to Dr. Johnson's house, 17 Gough Square, London, of which he was one of the original Governors. The house, which was occupied by Johnson during the years 1748-59, was bought by Cecil, Lord Harmsworth in 1911. On 3 January 1914 the *Times* reported that it had been fully restored and decorated and would shortly be open to the public. The caption not only parodies Johnson's ponderous phraseology, but also his moodiness, as exemplified in James Boswell's *Life of Samuel Johnson* (1791). There are some minor differences between the printed text and that written on the drawing.

tempus edax: devouring time; see Ovid, *Metamorphoses*, XV, 234: *tempus edax rerum*: O Time, thou great devourer. The phrase was used by Carlyle in his description of Johnson's house.

Lexiphanes: a bombastic speaker in the dialogue "Lexiphanes" by the Greek satirist Lucian (2nd century A.D.). The direct reference, however, is to a work entitled *Lexiphanes, A Dialogue. Imitated from Lucian, and suited to the present Times. . . . Being an attempt to restore the English Tongue to its ancient Purity, And to correct, as well as expose, the affected Style, hard Words, and absurd Phraseology of many late Writers, and particularly of Our English Lexiphanes, the Rambler.* . . . (London: J. Knox, 1767). The book was published anonymously by Archibald Campbell.

The Rambler, a periodical in 208 numbers, appeared from 20 March 1750 to 14 March 1752. With the exception of four numbers, they were all written by Johnson, when he lived in Gough Square. The verb *sublimify* does not occur in *The Rambler*, but the verb *sublime* does (13 November 1750).

One of Beerbohm's finest essays is "'A Clergyman'" (*AEN*, pp. 227-35), a meditation on Boswell's *Life*, combined with a parody of Johnson's style.

In the Shades—1915. 1915
Courtesy of Dr. Johnson's House Trust, London
HD 831

59

Boswell: Are you not pleased, Sir, that your house in Gough Square is to be presented to the Nation? Johnson: Why, no, Sir. You are to consider that the purpose of a house is to be inhabited by some one. If a house be not fit for tenancy by Tom or Dick, let it be demolished or handed over without more ado to the rats, which, by frequentation, will have acquired a prescriptive right there. I conceive that in Gough Square a vast number of rats will have been disturbed and evicted. (Puffing, and rolling himself from side to side.) Sir, I am sorry for the rats. Sir, the rats have a just grievance. Boswell: Nevertheless, Sir, is it not well that the house of the great Samuel Johnson should be preserved? Will it not tend to diffuse happiness and to promote virtue? Johnson: Nay, Sir, let us have no more of

this foppishmess. The house is naught. Let us not *sublimify* lath and plaster. I know not whether I profited the world while I was in it. I am very sure that my mere tenement will not be profitable now that I am out of it. Alas, Sir, when "tempus edax" has swallowed the yolk of the egg, there is no gain to be had by conservation of the egg-shell. 59

. . . or, (so very much was Lexiphanes a man of moods) the dialogue might run thus . . .

BOSWELL: Are you not glad, Sir, that your house in Gough Square is to be presented to the Nation? JOHNSON: Why, yes, Sir. (In a solemn, faltering tone.) Nothing has pleased me half so well since the *Rambler* was translated into the Russian language and read on the banks of the Wolga.

60 In this drawing John Morley (1838-1923), first Viscount of Blackburn, statesman and biographer, is seen introducing a pale, intellectual John Stuart Mill (1806-73) to Dante Gabriel Rossetti (1828-82), who is standing on the left. His reason for introducing them is their common "interest" in women, and he suggests that the artist illustrate Mill's *The Subjection of Women.*

In *The Subjection of Women* the author pleaded for equal rights for women. The book was published in 1869 and bitterly attacked. Its object was, in Mill's own words, to show that "the principle which regulates the existing social relations between the two sexes—the legal subordination of one sex to the other—is wrong in itself, and now one of the chief hindrances to human improvement; and that it ought to be replaced by a principle of perfect equality, admitting no power or privilege on the one side, nor disability on the other" (p. 1). Stanton Coit, the editor of *The Subjection of Women*, put it mildly when he said of Mill's style that his thought in this book seldom bends to "concrete instance, narrative, or historic and literary allusion."

The picture on the wall evokes Rossetti's later, more sensual manner; it may represent Jane Burden (cf. Surtees, plates 407-09, and passim as model). Rossetti met Jane Burden in Oxford in 1857 and introduced her to his friends, among them William Morris, who married her in April 1859.

For John Morley as biographer see plate 62; for D. G. Rossetti see plates 41-46, 48, 49, 55.

Mr. Morley of Blackburn, on an afternoon in the Spring of '69, introduces Mr. John Stuart Mill. 1917
Courtesy of the Tate Gallery, London
HD 1280

60

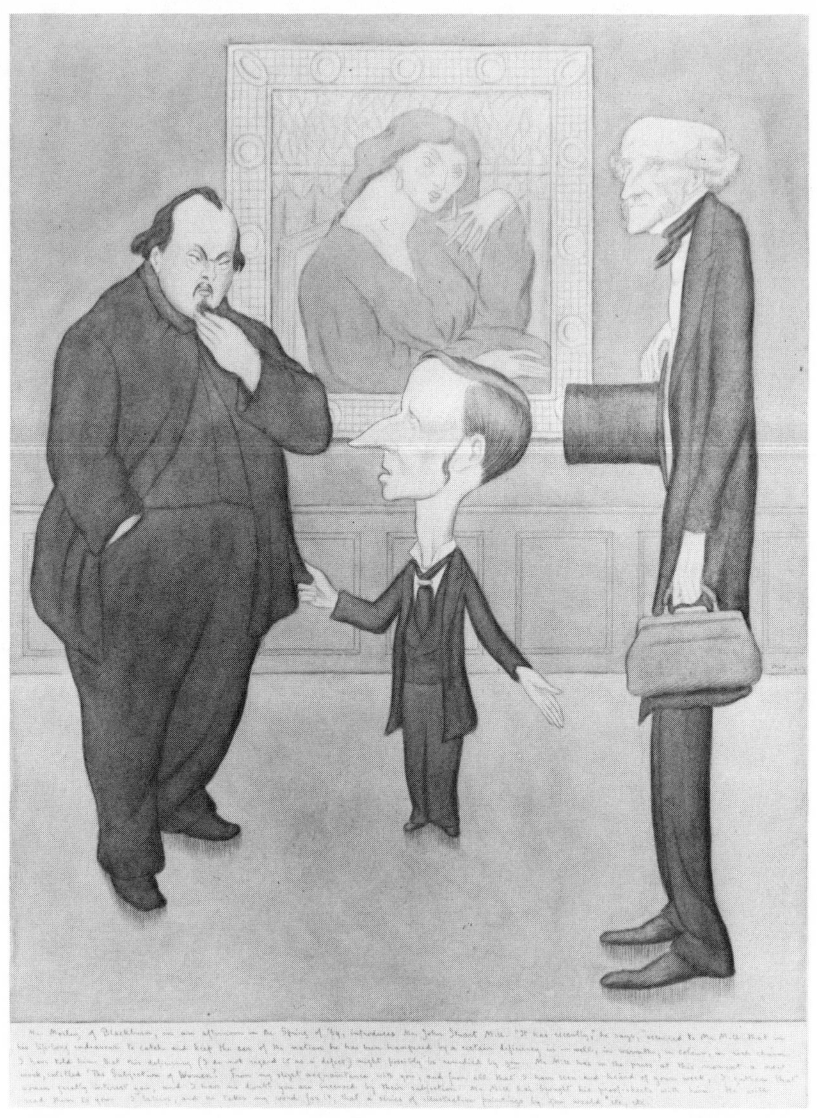

"It has recently," he says, "occurred to Mr. Mill that in his lifelong endeavour to catch and keep the ear of the nation he has been hampered by a certain deficiency in—well, in warmth, in colour, in rich charm. I have told him that this deficiency (I do not regard it as a defect) might possibly be remedied by *you*. Mr. Mill has in the press at this moment a new work, entitled 'The Subjection of

Women.' From my slight acquaintance with you, and from all that 60
I have seen and heard of your work, I gather that women greatly interest you, and I have no doubt that you are incensed at their subjection. Mr. Mill has brought his proof-sheets with him. He will read them to you. I believe, and he takes my word for it, that a series of illustrative paintings by you would" etc., etc.

61 The drawing represents Matthew Arnold (1822-88), the English poet and critic. "A little girl with a pigtail and the dark red dress of the period and her hands dutifully clasped behind her, looks up to the big man, lounging with a wide sardonic grin against the mantelpiece" (Lynch, p. 127). The little girl, Mary Augusta, granddaughter of Thomas Arnold of Rugby and a niece of Matthew Arnold, eventually became well known as Mrs. Humphry Ward (1851-1920), the novelist, author of the Victorian bestseller *Robert Elsmere* (1888).

The drawing plays on Matthew Arnold's theory of "high seriousness," a quality which he found missing in such poets as Chaucer and Burns (see, e.g., his essay on "The Study of Poetry"). But the subtle ambiguity of Beerbohm's wit is brought out by a remark like the following, made by a critic sixty years after the drawing was published: "What is still today irresistible is Arnold's gaiety, his wry astonishment at stupidity, his delighted amusement at folly, his instant recognition of distinction, and the urbane self-deprecating, faintly weary inflexion that does not for an instant conceal the hopeful and intense seriousness with which he approached the life that he saw about him" (*Matthew Arnold: Selected Essays*, ed. Noel Annan, p. xv).

Beerbohm much admired Arnold. In 1901 he expressed himself on the subject of Arnold's humor in these words: ". . . in Matthew Arnold's controversial writings the humorous passages are always distinct interludes or 'asides' consciously made, and distinct from the scheme of the essay. They are irresistible by reason of the preceding seriousness" (*AT*, p. 174; see also Cecil, p. 370).

According to Beerbohm, Mrs. Ward was mediocre, and therefore wrote dull books; also her *Eleanor* was too slow for good drama. She was rather "a critic, an essayist, working ably in another medium" (*MT*, p. 504, and pp. 461, 505).

Cf. plates 6 and 76.

The Poets' Corner (1904)
HD 37

61

MR. MATTHEW ARNOLD. TO HIM, MISS MARY AUGUSTA, HIS NIECE: "Why, Uncle Matthew, oh why, will not you be always wholly serious?" [1904]

62

John Morley, first Viscount of Blackburn (1838-1923), the English statesman and biographer, was chief secretary for Ireland in Gladstone's government. He wrote lives or studies of Burke, Voltaire, Rousseau, Diderot, Cobden, Walpole, and Cromwell. A year after the death of Gladstone in 1898, Morley began his work on the official biography of his old chief. *The Life of William Ewart Gladstone* was published in three thick volumes in 1903, the year in which Lord Rowton died. Gladstone's cobwebbed bust can be seen on top of the bookcase. See also plate 60.

Montagu William Lowry Corry, first Baron Rowton (1838-1903), the English politician and philanthropist, was private secretary to Disraeli until the latter's death in 1881. Interested in improving the dwellings of the working classes, he determined to establish "a poor man's hotel," which should offer better accommodation than the common lodging-houses at similar prices. The first "Rowton House" was opened at Vauxhall, London, in 1892, the cost (£30,000) being defrayed by Lord Rowton himself, though he was by no means a man of great wealth. Two years later a company, Rowton Houses (Limited), was incorporated to extend the scheme, a main characteristic of which was that the houses should not be charitable institutions but should be on a paying commercial basis. The scheme proved an immediate success, and was imitated not only in many of the principal towns of Great Britain, but also in Europe and America.

The Great Biography [?*c.* 1901]
Courtesy of the Ashmolean Museum, Oxford
HD 1066

62

LORD ROWTON TO MR. MORLEY: "My *dear* Sir, why spend three years in writing a Life, when you can spend twenty in *not* writing it? Come! Build a Model Lodging-House!"

63 Early in 1876 certain English poets tried to introduce the French forms of Villon, Marot, and Théodore de Banville into English verse. Henry Austin Dobson (1840-1921), poet and biographer, was at the head of this movement, and in May 1876 he published in "The Prodigals" the first original "ballade" written in English.

Austin Dobson and his friend Edmund William Gosse (1849-1928), critic and poet, both served in the Board of Trade, the former as a clerk, the latter as a translator, when Joseph Chamberlain, the Radical politician, was President of it (1880-85). (For Max's caricatures of Chamberlain see HD 270-285A.) An American observer described the Board of Trade in those days as "a Nest of Singing Birds." In the drawing a "ballade" is seen evolving from Dobson's head. Gosse published two essays on Austin Dobson's life and works.

Beerbohm had started a sonnet game in which he and a friend wrote alternate lines on an agreed-upon theme. "To Henry James" (*MV*, p. 19) is an example of this game played with Edmund Gosse; see also SC 286.

The Gosse correspondence, preserved in the Brotherton Library, Leeds, comprises twenty-two letters by Max Beerbohm to Edmund Gosse; see A. Whitworth, *et al.*, *A Catalogue of the Gosse Correspondence in the Brotherton Collection* (Leeds: The Brotherton Library, 1950). *The Life and Letters of Sir Edmund Gosse* by Evan Charteris contains several letters written to Beerbohm by Gosse.

The text on the drawing reads: " . . . Mr. Austin Dobson and Mr. Edmund Gosse caught in the act of composing a ballade by their President . . . "

See plates 47 and 64.

Courtesy of the Ashmolean Museum, Oxford
HD 442

63

Scene: The Board of Trade. Time: Office hours in the early eighties [1904]

Mr. Austin Dobson and Mr. Edmund Gosse, composing a ballade, are taken unawares by their President, Mr. Jos. Chamberlain.

64 One of a series of drawings entitled "The Old and the Young Self," published in *Observations*; see plate 26. The persons, from left to right, are: Lord Londonderry (1878-1949), Lytton Strachey (1880-1932), J. C. Squire (1884-1958), Edward Shanks (1892-1953), W. B. Yeats (1865-1939), Maurice Baring (1874-1945), Randall Thomas Davidson, Archbishop of Canterbury (1848-1930), Edward Howard Marsh (1872-1953), Lord Lincolnshire (1843-1928), Lord Crewe (1858-1945), Arthur Wing Pinero (1855-1934), R. B. Haldane (1856-1928), Robert Bridges (1844-1930), Evan Charteris (1864-1940), and Herbert Asquith (1881-1947).

Edmund Gosse was the son of the distinguished zoologist Philip Henry Gosse, who was a Plymouth Brother and religious bigot. As a result, Edmund Gosse was brought up in an atmosphere of rigid piety. In 1907 he published *Father and Son: A Study of Two Temperaments*, in which, among other things, he describes his admission into the communion of the "Saints." Gosse was made C.B. in 1912, and knighted in 1925.

"Gosse went in for being a host. His parties were not always agreeable. There were often too many people for the room: sometimes the entertainment provided failed to please" (Cecil, p. 152).

Rupert Hart-Davis records an undated caricature of "Edmund Gosse in a Cavalry Mess" (HD 619). Pasted on to various parts of this drawing are printed excerpts from a "pen sketch" of Gosse: "He has outgrown his early delicacy . . . is tall . . . blue eyes, at least so far as I could judge through his eye-glasses . . . well-furnished with, it goes without saying, an intellectual head . . . and, to complete the inventory, a heavy fair moustache . . . encyclopaedic learning . . . "

Max did several other caricatures of Edmund Gosse (see HD 610-621A). He had copies of a number of Gosse's books in his library (SC 86-94). He reviewed Gosse's *Ibsen*, published in 1907 (*LT*, pp. 351-54), and parodied his thought and style in "A Recollection" (*CG*, pp. 119-30).

See plates 21, 31, 32, 35, 47, 51, 63, 75, 76, 102

The Old and the Young Self: Sir Edmund Gosse, C. B. 1924
Courtesy of the Ashmolean Museum, Oxford
HD 616

64

Young Self: "Are you saved?"

65 In this drawing Cunninghame Graham's Young Self, riding a rocking-horse, greets the Old Self, leaping in through the window as a centaur.

Robert Bontine Cunninghame Graham (1852-1936), traveler, poet, horseman, scholar, Scottish nationalist, ardent socialist, and friend of "Buffalo Bill," was the author of studies of old Spanish life and the *conquistadores*, and of a large number of stories, essays, and sketches. His travel books include *Mogreb-el-Acksa* (1898), *El Rio de la Plata* (1914), and *Cartagena and the Banks of the Sinu* (1920). His best-known stories and sketches are collected in *Thirteen Stories* (1900), *Success* (1902), *Faith* (1909), *Hope* (1910), *Charity* (1912), and *Scottish Stories* (1914).

Cunninghame Graham went to Buenos Aires when he was seventeen, and spent most of the years between 1870 and 1878 in South America, where he learnt about ranching and the *gaucho* life. Afterwards he stayed in Texes, and explored the plains of Venezuela on horseback. When he was in Paris, he preferred a prancing horse to a *fiacre* as a means of getting about the city, and when he became an M.P., he regularly rode to the House of Commons on his favorite horse. He did not start writing until he was well over forty. He was one of the great horsemen of his day and wrote well about horses. He died in Buenos Aires.

Graham looked like a Spanish Don, and people were often reminded of Don Quixote when they saw him. A reporter once described him as "a striking figure, with a breezy head of hair and moustachios to match, and a sharply pointed beard, lighter than his hair." The portrait of Charles Gould in Joseph Conrad's *Nostromo* is based partly on Cunninghame Graham.

Referring to Cunninghame Graham's (then) recently published travel book *Mogreb-el-Acksa*, Beerbohm wrote him in 1899: "I have been revelling in 'Mogreb-el-Acksa,' certain passage of which I know by heart. It is refreshing and delightful to have such a book, and I firmly demand another" (Polwarth).

Beerbohm owned copies of four of Graham's books, all inscribed or signed by the author (SC 95).

The Old and the Young Self: Mr. Cunninghame Graham. 1924
Observations (1925)
HD 628

65

66 As editor of the *Fortnightly Review* and owner-editor of the *Saturday Review*, James Thomas ("Frank") Harris (1856-1931), author and adventurer, encouraged the best writers of his generation. He encouraged the young Beerbohm to write for the *Saturday Review*, which resulted in his becoming dramatic critic on that weekly in 1898.

Harris's most popular book is his pornographic autobiography *My Life and Loves*, which he wrote at the end of his life (5 vols., 1922-58, the last volume by Alexander Trocchi, based on unpublished material by Frank Harris).

In Harris's own opinion, one of the disappointments in his life was the conviction of his personal ugliness and the fact that he was too short and small to be a great fighter or athlete. Max represents him "preened and inflated like a fighting cock, as if to signify his sexual activity and self-confidence" (Felstiner 1973, p. 115). "Stocky, red-faced, with rolling eyes and a huge curling moustache which he hoped made him look like Bismarck, [Harris] was an adventurer who had during the 'eighties burst upon the literary world of England like a tornado. He was a cad, a liar and a professional amorist, all three on a heroic scale; also a brilliant, picturesque talker, with a considerable gift for writing—he later produced a lively and controversial book about the character of Shakespeare—and a wonderful flair as an editor. . . . when in after-years someone asked [Beerbohm] if Frank Harris ever spoke the truth, 'Sometimes, don't you know,' said Max, 'when his invention flagged' " (Cecil, p. 164).

In the Robert H. Taylor Collection in the Princeton University Library there is a copy of Max's *Caricatures of Twenty-Five Gentlemen* (1896) in which the artist, years after publication, has written on the blank page facing this drawing of Harris: "Not forcible enough in pose. The right arm should have been outstretched and the fist clenched. F. H. was always far more dynamic than he looks here" (Felstiner 1972, p. 79, and fig. 10).

Beerbohm parodied Harris's thought and style in "Shakespeare and Christmas" (*CG*, pp. 67-73). Harris had an absorbing interest in Shakespeare: in 1909 he published *The Man Shakespeare*, a provocative book about the character of the Bard. (A year later Max drew a mock

Mr. Frank Harris [1896]
Caricatures of Twenty-Five Gentlemen (1896)
HD 711

66

Mr Frank Harris Max

frontispiece for "that work of brilliant and profound criticism," HD 66
716.) Cecil (p. 164) relates how one day in 1896 Max was Harris's guest at a luncheon. "During a moment of silence Harris's voice was heard booming out: 'Unnatural vice!' he was saying, 'I know nothing of the joys of unnatural vice. You must ask my friend Oscar about them. But,' he went on, with a reverential change of tone, 'had Shakespeare asked me, I should have had to submit!' Max went home and drew a cartoon of Harris, stark naked and with his moustache bristling, looking coyly over his shoulder at Shakespeare who shrinks back at the alarming prospect." Underneath the (undated) drawing is written: "Had Shakespeare asked me . . . " (HD 720; see also SC 108).

On 3 November 1900 Beerbohm reviewed a performance of Harris's *Mr. and Mrs. Daventry* (*MT*, pp. 310-14). In 1902 he collaborated with Harris in adapting Paul Hervieu's *L'Énigme* as *Caesar's Wife* (see Beerbohm's review of this play in *MT*, pp. 443-44). Harris's *Contemporary Portraits: Fourth Series* (1924) contains an essay on Beerbohm entitled "The Incomparable." In a letter to the Editor of the *Times Literary Supplement* of 28 February 1924, p. 128, Max objected to an anecdote in this book.

Max owned a copy of the first edition of Harris's *The Bomb* (1908), inscribed to him by the author (SC 109).

67 Beerbohm's lifelong aversion to Rudyard Kipling (1865-1936) arose from his feeling that Kipling was debasing his genius by what he wrote. He detested the vulgarity, or rather vulgarization, of Kipling's true talent, and therefore he pursued him relentlessly in caricatures—HD lists as many as twenty-six!—critical articles, and one brilliant parody of his thought and style, "P. C., X, 36" (*CG*, pp. 9-17). A "belligerent jaw thrust out above a jerky, inadequate body" (Felstiner 1973, p. 159) is an inevitable aspect of Kipling in Beerbohm's caricatures.

There was to Beerbohm "something hysterical, perverse and even feminine in Kipling's strident admiration for mere maleness. Could his name be a pseudonym for a female author, Max asked wickedly; for surely real men take masculinity more for granted. He hated Kipling's apparent approval of the brute and the bully, 'the smell of blood, beer and "baccy"', which, he said, exhaled from Kipling's pages" (Cecil, p. 251).

When, in 1907, Kipling had just been made a D.Litt. of Oxford, Max protested against this on the ground that "'the idols of the market-place need no wreaths from an university.' According to him a university might fittingly crown a writer 'whose mastery does but win him the quiet homage of the finer critics'" (Riewald 1953, p. 29).

In the Robert H. Taylor Collection in the Princeton University Library there is a copy of Max's *Caricatures of Twenty-Five Gentlemen* (1896) in which the artist, years after publication, has emended this drawing on the blank page facing it, correcting the back of Kipling's neck to make it, according to his annotation, "more brutal" (Felstiner 1972, p. 79, and fig. 8).

Beerbohm owned a copy of Kipling's *Barrack-Room Ballads* (1892) and of *A Diversity of Creatures* (1917). On the title-page of the latter book he has written under the author's name: "the Apocalypic [*sic*] Bounder who can do such fine things but mostly prefers to stand (on tip-toe and stridently) for all that is cheap and nasty" (SC 136, 137).

See plates 68-72.

Mr. Rudyard Kipling [1896]
Caricatures of Twenty-Five Gentlemen (1896)
HD 850

67

Mr Rudyard Kipling

68 The references in the caption are to Tennyson's poem "The Charge of the Heavy Brigade at Balaclava, October 25, 1854"; to Sir Lewis Morris (1833-1907), the popular poet and Welsh educationist, whose *The Epic of Hades* (1876-77) reached some forty-five editions during the author's lifetime; and to Alfred Charles William Harmsworth, Viscount Northcliffe (1865-1922), journalist, and proprietor of the imperialist *Daily Mail* and other newspapers. "The emphasis of 'wholesomeness' is a reminder of how much Kipling owed, indirectly, to the national disgust at the Wilde scandal of 1895. Kipling's manly vigor seemed to John Bull just the proper antidote" (McElderry 1972, p. 134).

See plates 67, 69-72.

The drawing shows a well-fed and rosy John Bull in a pub, congratulating his poet Rudyard Kipling. The poet appears in a Norfolk jacket, knickers, and a cricket cap, smoking a clay pipe, and flourishing a frothy mug of beer. The decrepit and querulous old John is drawing on a long-stemmed pipe. A diminutive puppy is sitting on its hindlegs in token of submission. Some think it represents Alfred Austin, the Poet Laureate.

The caption imitates Kipling's style.

De Arte Poetica [1901]
Cartoons "The Second Childhood of John Bull" (1911)
HD 1875

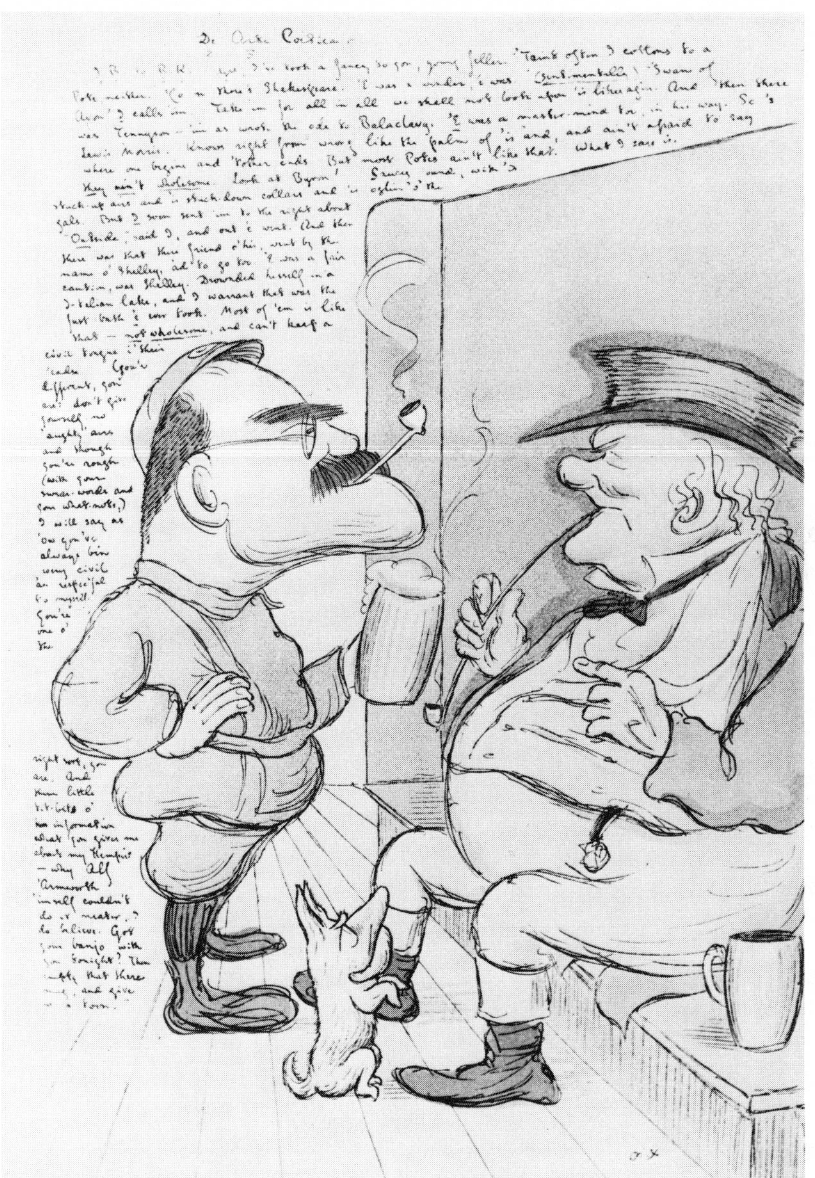

68

DE ARTE POETICA. *J.B. to R.K.* "Yes, I've took a fancy to you, young feller. 'Tain't often I cottons to a Pote, neither. 'Course there's Shakespeare. 'E was a wonder, 'e was (*sentimentally*). 'Swan of Avon' *I* calls 'im. Take 'im for all in all we shall not look upon 'is

likes agin. And then there was Tennyson—'im as wrote the ode to Balaclavy. 'E was a master-mind too, in his way. So's Lewis Morris. Knows right from wrong like the palm of 'is 'and, and ain't afraid to say where one begins and t'other ends. But most potes ain't like that. What I say is, *they ain't wholesome.* Look at Byron! Saucy 'ound, with 'is stuck-up airs and 'is stuck-down collars and 'is oglin' o' the gals. But *I* soon sent 'im to the right about. '*Outside,*' said I, and out 'e went. And then there was that there friend o' his, went by the name o' Shelley, 'ad to go too. 'E was a fair caution, was Shelley. Drownded hisself in a I-talian lake, and I warrant that was the fust bath 'e ever took. Most of 'em is like that—*not wholesome,* and can't keep a civil tongue i' their 'eads. You're different, you are: don't give yourself no 'aughty airs, and though you're rough (with your swear-words and your what-nots), I will say as 'ow you've always bin very civil an' respec'ful to myself. You're one o' the right sort, you are. And them little tit-bits o' information what you gives me about my Hempire—why Alf 'armsworth 'imself couldn't do it neater, I do believe. Got your banjo with you to-night? Then empty that there mug, and give us a toon." 68

69 "The Absent-Minded Beggar" is one of Kipling's banjo melodies on the subject of Tommy Atkins. The rhyme is about the soldiers out on active service in the Boer War (1899-1902), and the families they had to leave behind.

In a letter written in 1913 to Holbrook Jackson, author of *The Eighteen Nineties,* Beerbohm sums up his attitude to Kipling the Poet: "To me, who gets the finest of all literary joy out of Henry James (his middle and late manners), the sort of person that Kipling is, and the sort of thing that Kipling does, cannot strongly appeal—quite the contrary. I carefully guard myself by granting you that Kipling is a genius. Indeed, even *I* can't help *knowing* him to be that. The *schoolboy,* the *bounder,* and the *brute*—these three types have surely never found a more brilliant expression of themselves than in R.K. (Nor, will I further grant, has the *nursery*-maid.) But as a poet and a seer R.K. seems to me not to exist, except for the purpose of contempt. All the ye-ing and the Lord-God-ing and the Law-ing side of him seems to me a very thin and trumpery assumption; and I have always thought it was a sound impulse by which he was driven to put his 'Recessional' into the waste-paper basket, and a great pity that Mrs. Kipling fished it out and made him send it to *The Times.* I think (absurd tho' it is to prophesy) that futurity will give him among poets a place corresponding exactly with the place reserved for Theodore Roosevelt among statesmen" (Cecil, pp. 321-22).

The drawing represents Kipling in an empty monastic cell, holding a quill pen; the caption reads: "Scenes from the Lives of the Poets." The inscription on the back wall, "VOS PANDITE VATI PIERIDES" (Reveal yourselves, ye Muses, to the bard) is from Claudius Claudianus, *In Rufinum,* I, 23-24.

See plates 67, 68, 70-72.

Mr. Rudyard Kipling composing "The Absent-Minded Beggar" [1903]

Courtesy of the Department of Printing and Graphic Arts, Harvard College Library

HD 854

69

Max
Scenes from the Lives of the Poets –
Rudyard Kipling
composing "The
Absent-Minded
Beggar" –

70 The drawing shows "a prancing, determined looking Kipling, blowing a tin horn and wearing a Greek helmet. On his arm is a tall, lithe and young Britannia, dressed in a flowing classical gown and wearing Kipling's bowler" (Stevenson, p. 110).

The caption imitates the tone and style of many of Kipling's poems. The reference is to Hampstead Heath, in the northwest of London. With its broken heights, its grassy glades, and its far-reaching views, Hampstead Heath was the finest of London's open spaces in the early decades of this century. The phrase "the blasted 'eath" is taken from Shakespeare's *Macbeth,* I, iii, 75-78:

> Say from whence
> You owe this strange intelligence? or why
> Upon this blasted heath you stop our way
> With such prophetic greeting?

Beerbohm parodied Kipling's poetry in "After Kipling's *Barrack-Room Ballads,*" "After Kipling's 'Recessional'", and "Addition to Kipling's 'The Dead King (Edward VII.), 1910'" (*MV*, pp. 16, 125, 126).

See plates 67-69, 71, 72.

The Poets' Corner (1904)
HD 855

70

Mr. Rudyard Kipling takes a bloomin' day aht, on the blasted 'eath, along with Britannia, 'is gurl. [1904]

71 One of a series of drawings entitled "The Old and the Young Self," published in *Observations*; see plate 26.

On the right is an impression of the young Kipling in India, in a topee. On the left he appears as the unofficial poet laureate—he had just missed the laureateship after Tennyson's death in 1892—, laden with honors, including the Nobel Prize, which he got in 1907. The background is filled with the paraphernalia of empire.

Mrs. Hauksbee, one of Kipling's best women characters, is the chief person in eight of his early stories, and is mentioned in two others. The first story about Mrs. Hauksbee, "Three—and an Extra," was published in 1886. The best of all the Mrs. Hauksbee stories is "Mrs. Hauksbee Sits Out," published in 1890.

According to Beerbohm, the dramatization of Kipling's novel *The Light That Failed* by "George Fleming" (Julia Constance Fletcher) showed all the faults of its original: the exaggerated "manlydom" of his male characters (which even might lead one to suppose that "Rudyard Kipling" was a lady's pseudonym) and "that abrupt jargon of alternate meiosis and hyperbole" which constituted his literary style (*AT*, pp. 245-49).

See plates 67-70, 72.

The Old and the Young Self: Mr. Rudyard Kipling. 1924
Courtesy of the Department of Printing and Graphic Arts, Harvard College Library
HD 861

71

YOUNG SELF: "I *say*! Have you heard the latest about Mrs. Hauksbee?"

72 An "improved" portrait of Kipling occurring in Beerbohm's copy of Richard Le Gallienne's *Rudyard Kipling: A Criticism*, with a bibliography by John Lane, published in 1900 (SC 139). The book is inscribed on the fly-leaf by the author: "For Max, from Dick. June 1900." The portrait has been worked on by Max and finally transformed into a bitterly satiric caricature full of loathing, and the title changed from "Rudyard Kipling" to "Rudyard Kipling's Soul." Felstiner (1973, p. 98) describes the drawing in these words: "Kipling has a cleft chin, idiot sneer, and eyes jerking sideways as if in panic."

Once Beerbohm and Kipling passed each other in a hansom in the Strand. Beerbohm saw him and Kipling knew that Beerbohm had seen him. But as the hansoms passed, they each of them averted their eyes. Some years later, when he saw Kipling at a London club, Max had the impulse to go to him and say: "Mr. Kipling, I admire you. I admire your very great genius. If I have written harshly of you, it is because I do not believe you are living up to the possibilities of your genius." But he didn't go over to him, and when Max, in his old age, told Behrman about this incident, he added: "And now he is dead and it is too late" (Behrman, p. 71).

For Richard Le Gallienne see plates 51 and 58; see further plates 67-71.

Rudyard Kipling's Soul [n.d.]

Catalogue of the Library and Literary Manuscripts of the late Sir Max Beerbohm. Illustrated edition (1960)

not in HD

72

73 When Max made this drawing, Bertrand Russell (1872-1970), the English philosopher, had already published a large number of books on logic, philosophy, sociology, and politics. In 1924 his reputation mainly rested—as it still does—on two studies dealing with the foundations of logic, *The Principles of Mathematics* (1903) and *Principia Mathematica* (1910-13; with A. N. Whitehead). Among his philosophical works published before 1924, the year in which the drawing was made, are *The Problems of Philosophy* (1912), *Our Knowledge of the External World as a Field for Scientific Method in Philosophy* (1914), and *The Analysis of Mind* (1921). Russell's social and political writings then included *Principles of Social Reconstruction* (1916), *Political Ideals* (1917), *Roads to Freedom: Socialism, Anarchism, and Syndicalism* (1918), *The Practice and Theory of Bolshevism* (1920), and *The Problem of China* (1922). At the time of drawing this caricature, Beerbohm may have known about two of Russell's books on science: *The ABC of Atoms* (1923), and *Icarus; or, the Future of Science* (1924).

In this drawing the three Sciences and Politics are represented by sexless creatures in white robes, three of them spectacled. Logic's "dear Mr. Mill" refers to John Stuart Mill (1806-73), the English philosopher, author of *A System of Logic* (1843); see plate 60.

Bertrand Russell, on the occasion of Beerbohm's eightieth birthday, published an article entitled "'The Faultless Max' at 80," in the *New York Times Magazine* of 24 August 1952, pp. 18-19.

Logic and Mathematics reconciled through the bitterness of beholding the passionate advances now made by Mr. Bertrand Russell to Physics. 1924

Observations (1925)

HD 1346

73

LOGIC: "How unlike dear Mr. Mill!"—MATHEMATICS: "Odiously incontinual and fluxional!"—POLITICS: "He even had the impertinence to flirt with *me* once. And no man ever understood me less well."

74

Walter de la Mare (1873-1956), the English lyrical poet and writer of stories for children, was only four years old when his father died. He was brought up by his mother, who had a great influence on him and from whom he heard many of the legends and fairy tales which he later used in his work. The magical mixture of realism and fantasy which characterizes his poems and stories is the result of his awareness that there may be a mystery behind the commonest experience.

As Dr. F. R. Leavis has remarked, de la Mare's "most successful stories derive from the same kind of impulse as his poetry," though "the sharp critical awareness that guides him in his poetry does not function here" (*New Bearings,* p. 55). The drawing captures the atmosphere evoked by a poem like the following:

Which?

"What did you say?"
"I? Nothing." "No? . . .
What was that sound?"
"When?"
"Then."
"I do not know."
"Whose eyes were those on us?"
"Where?"
"There."
"No eyes I saw."
"Speech, footfall, presence—how cold the night may be!"
"Phantom or fantasy, it's all one to *me.*"

The Complete Poems of Walter de la Mare, p. 385.

Beerbohm owned a copy of the first edition of de la Mare's *The Riddle and Other Stories* (1923), inscribed to him by the author (SC 56).

Courtesy of the Ashmolean Museum, Oxford
HD 423

74

Mr. Walter de la Mare gaining inspiration for an eerie and lovely story. 1925

75 This drawing, dated November 1920, was exhibited at the Leicester Galleries, London, in May-June 1921; the text on it reads: " . . . trying hard to see her. . . . " Max's footnote "—and contriving—M. B. 1921" was added in the Leicester Galleries catalogue after Lytton Strachey's *Queen Victoria* was published.

William Lamb, second Viscount Melbourne (1779-1848), was Prime Minister in 1834, and from 1835 to 1841. He was the intimate adviser and daily companion of the young Queen Victoria during the first four years of her reign.

Giles Lytton Strachey (1880-1932) published his *Queen Victoria* on 7 April 1921. On 20 June of that year Beerbohm wrote to his friend Reggie Turner: "Have you read Lytton Strachey's *Queen Victoria*? That I *am* a Stoic is proved by my having no jealousy of him at all, though his mind and his prose are so like mine and so exactly like what I should have loved mine to be" (*LRT*, p. 259).

Many years later, in his Rede Lecture, Max expressed himself in these words: " . . . aren't there in the Elysian Fields two other worthies who have reason to be grateful to the supposed iconoclast?—Queen Victoria and the Prince Consort? The Prince in his life-time had never been popular; and after Sir Theodore Martin's saccharine biography he had become a veritable mock. I never heard a kind word for him. The Queen, who in my childhood and youth had been not only revered but worshipped, was, soon after her death, no longer in public favour. Her faults had become known, and her virtues were unheeded. This is not so now; and is not so by reason of Lytton Strachey's fully judicial presentment of her with all the faults over which her virtues so very much preponderated. And it is, by the same token, through him that we know the Prince not as just dreadfully admirable, but as some one to be loved and to be sorry for" (*LS*, pp. 19-20).

Theodore Martin's "saccharine" biography, *Queen Victoria as I Knew Her,* was issued for private circulation in 1901, and published in 1908. Beerbohm owned a copy of the latter edition, bought for sixpence by Philip Guedalla and presented to him as "a reminder of the changed values of a later age" (SC 148).

See plates 64 and 76.

Courtesy of the National Gallery of Victoria, Melbourne
HD 1602

75

Mr. Lytton Strachey, trying* to see her with Lord Melbourne's eyes.
November 1920

*—and contriving—
M. B. 1921

76 This drawing is a pictorial and verbal echo of the caricature in which Matthew Arnold's niece, Mary Augusta, asks her uncle why he will not be always wholly serious (see plate 61). The design on the wallpaper is made up of heads of Queen Victoria and other Eminent Victorians.

In 1943 the University of Cambridge honored Beerbohm by asking him to deliver the Rede Lecture for that year. He spoke on Lytton Strachey, whose work he overrated. The lecture was published that same year. Strachey's biography of Dr. Thomas Arnold of Rugby had appeared in *Eminent Victorians* (1918). Of this biography Max said in his lecture: "In the character of Dr. Arnold there was such a wealth of grit, and a strenuousness so terrific that one may rather wonder how Strachey could bear to think of him and write of him. The portrait fails, I think, because it is composed throughout in a vein of sheer mockery. It is the only work of his that does not seek, does not hesitate, does not penetrate, and is definitely unfair. It is the only work of his that might, so far as it goes, justify the application to him of that term [*scil.* 'debunker'] which shall not again soil my lips and afflict your ears" (*LS*, pp. 11-12). Of Strachey's *Elizabeth and Essex* (1928) Max once said "that it was a 'brave' thing for Strachey to have tried but that, at best, it was only 'guesswork'" (Behrman, p. 283).

Strachey died on 21 January 1932. On 13 March of that year William Rothenstein wrote to Max: "I hated Lytton Strachey dying—one tilted at him, but he was one of the real men of his time" (*MW*, p. 141).

Beerbohm's library contained a copy of the first edition of Lytton Strachey's *Eminent Victorians,* with the title-page "improved" by him by the addition of a printed colored illustration of an elegantly dressed man with walking stick and gloves, inscribed by him, imitating Strachey's hand: "Yours very truly Lytton Strachey." He also owned first editions of three of Strachey's other books (SC 215-18).

For Strachey on Beerbohm see Holroyd, II, pp. 244-45 and 392-94. See further plates 64 and 75, and cf. plate 6.

Echo. 1923

Courtesy of the Birmingham Museums and Art Gallery

HD 1603

76

"Why, Uncle Lytton, oh why . . . "

77 According to one of their biographers, Sir Osbert Sitwell (1892-1969), his brother Sacheverell (born 1897), and their sister Dame Edith (1887-1964) formed "an extraordinary trio . . . of poets and personages" (Mégroz, p. 56). But Dr. F. R. Leavis was of a different opinion. According to him the Sitwells belonged to "the history of publicity rather than of poetry" (*New Bearings*, p. 73).

The drawing shows "Osbert in white tie and tails and Sacheverell in dinner jacket address[ing] one another through the parrots perched on their respective wrists in mutual laudation" (Lehmann, p. 61). The words issuing from the parrots' mouths are "Bravo, Sacheverell!," "Well done, Osbert!"

Osbert's five-volume autobiography, *Left Hand, Right Hand* (1944-50), amply testifies to his devoted admiration for his younger brother. Though he was separated by five years from Sacheverell, "they were constant companions; from earliest youth he delighted in the quick and merry flashes of his younger brother's intelligence" (Fulford, p. 6). Max also emphasizes the likeness between the two Sitwell brothers, which was indeed striking: they were "about six feet in height, and blond. They . . . [had] the long, sharp-featured face, high-bridged nose, straight, pale hair and light eyes—grey, grey-blue and grey-green—of a well recognised type" (Mégroz, p. 55).

On one occasion the two brothers cooperated in writing a book. In 1927 they published *All at Sea: A Social Tragedy in Three Acts for First-class Passengers Only,* with a preface entitled "A Few Days in an Author's Life" by Osbert Sitwell. The play was produced, under the title *First-class Passengers Only,* at the Arts Theatre Club, London, on 27 November 1927.

Max did five other drawings of the Sitwell brothers. One (HD 1549) has the caption: "Talis Amyclaeos non junxit gratia fratres" (No such grace united the Amyclaean brothers, i.e., Castor and Pollux).

Beerbohm owned presentation copies of the first editions of ten of Osbert and Sacheverell Sitwell's books, all inscribed by their authors to Max, or to Max and Florence Beerbohm (SC 206-07).

Mr. Osbert, and Mr. Sacheverell, Sitwell. 1923
Things New and Old (1923)
HD 1545

77

Part Seven

Novelists

78. Let Justice be Done
79. Leo Tolstoy
80. Henry James
81. Henry James (in America)
82. Henry James (in London)
83. The Old Pilgrim
84. Hall Caine
85. Somewhere in the Pacific
86. Conrad Again
87. The Old and the Young Self: Joseph Conrad
88. George Moore
89. George Moore
90. Rentrée of George Moore
91. The Old and the Young Self: George Moore
92. Maurice Hewlett
93. Robert Hichens
94. H. G. Wells
95. The Old and the Young Self: H. G. Wells
96. A Milestone
97. H. G. Wells and Arnold Bennett
98. The Old and the Young Self: Arnold Bennett
99. "Stephen Hudson"
100. A Flask of Bombarolina
101. Reginald Turner
102. The Old and the Young Self: Maurice Baring
103. A. S. M. Hutchinson
104. Aldous Huxley

78 Clement King Shorter (1857-1926), the English journalist and author, published his *Charlotte Brontë and Her Circle* in 1896; this was followed by *Charlotte Brontë and Her Sisters* (1905) and *The Brontës: Life and Letters* (1908); he also edited their works. Shorter's autobiography shows him to have been a happy man, happy in his unthinking energy, enjoying controversy, naive, and affectionate.

Sir Alexander Nelson Hood (1854-1937), Duke of Brontë, held family estates in Sicily—the historical Duchy of Brontë, with the title conferred on Lord Nelson by the King of Naples after the Battle of the Nile. The fact that Clement Shorter was the author of two books on Napoleon, *Napoleon and his Fellow-Travellers* (1908) and *Napoleon in his own Defence* (1910), may, for Max, have added zest to the imagined scene.

Beerbohm must have known that the family name of the Brontës was originally Brunty, a probable corruption of O'Prunty. The Rev. Patrick Brontë, the father of the Brontë sisters, adopted the name of Brontë soon after Nelson, whom he greatly admired, was made Duke of Brontë in 1799.

The picture in the background is a free rendering of Patrick Branwell Brontë's well-known painting of his sisters Anne (on left), Emily (in center), and Charlotte (on right), now in the National Portrait Gallery, London.

Let Justice be Done [n. d.]
Observations (1925)
HD 1521

78

MR. CLEMENT SHORTER (to MR. ALEXANDER NELSON HOOD): "And so you're the Duke of Brontë! Now do, like a good fellow, go and pull a wire or two at Court, and get Lottie and Em and Annie made Duchesses in retrospect!"

79 One of Beerbohm's "Misleading Frontispieces" (SC 228). The portrait of Leo Tolstoy (1828-1910), the Russian novelist and social critic, has been grotesquely altered, so that the Count has come to resemble a "Tartar-looking personage with eyeglass, plumed cap, and a gay, arch leer in his eye" (Cecil, p. 373). On the facing tissue Beerbohm has written: "'There were those who said that Tolstoi was self-conscious. It would be more just to say that he was conscious of himself.' Aylmer Maude." The drawing is here published for the first time.

The "improvement" is not dated, but Tolstoy's *What is Art?* appeared in 1898. That same year Aylmer Maude (1858-1938), Tolstoy's biographer and translator, published a translation of it in a periodical entitled *The New Order*. Shortly afterwards the translation appeared in book form. The Thomas Y. Crowell edition, in which the "improvement" occurs, is not dated, and there is no copy of it in the British Library or the Library of Congress. But judging from the type and binding, it must have been published about 1900.

Beerbohm condemned Tolstoy for holding that "the highest art is that which gives the greatest pleasure to the greatest number of uneducated persons" (*MT*, p. 226). He once referred to Tolstoy as an "inspired ass."

On 31 December 1904 Beerbohm attacked Louise and Aylmer Maude's translation of Tolstoy's play *The Power of Darkness* in the *Saturday Review*. Shaw challenged Max in a letter to the editor of this weekly, 14 January 1905, p. 48, and Max returned to the attack in his article "Dramatic Translation," 21 January 1905 (*LT*, pp. 113-16, 121-24). This exchange of views sparked off an untitled drawing, which Hart-Davis describes as follows: "[*A few bogus musical notes*] To G. B. S. from Max. Saturday, January 14, 1905 [.] *A modern version of the fight in Act IV of Gounod's 'Faust.'* Valentine Max, angry brother of Marguerite Tolstoy [*attacks*] Aylmer Faust, betrayer of Marguerite Tolstoy, [*with*] Mephisto Bernard, influential friend of Aylmer Faust [*as referee and*] Marguerite Tolstoy [*in background*]" (HD 1484).

Leo Tolstoy [n. d.]
Owner: J. G. Riewald
not in HD

79

80 Beerbohm was among the first who reacted intelligently and seriously to the work of the American novelist Henry James (1843-1916). They knew each other for twenty years, and between 1898 and 1954 Max did nineteen major caricatures of him (HD 801-18), wrote a number of parodies of his work, and reviewed two of his plays, *Guy Domville* (*MT*, pp. 307-08) and *The High Bid* (*AT*, pp. 540-45). He got "the finest of all literary joy out of Henry James (his middle and later manner)" (Cecil, p. 321), and thought *The Golden Bowl* and *The Wings of the Dove* his greatest and richest achievement.

The caricature was inspired by James's essay on D'Annunzio. At the end of this essay, written in the autumn of 1903, James "uses a striking image to characterize the emptiness of novels that isolate the physical from the act of living":

> Shut out from the rest of life, shut out from all fruition and assimilation, it has no more dignity than—to use a homely image—the boots and shoes that we see, in the corridors of promiscuous hotels, standing, often in double pairs, at the doors of rooms. Detached and unassociated these clusters of objects present, however obtruded, no importance. What the participants do with their agitation, in short, or even what it does with them, *that* is the stuff of poetry, and it is never really interesting save when something finely contributive in themselves makes it so.

"This passage would lead Max Beerbohm to draw one of his celebrated cartoons of Henry James. He would portray the bewildered novelist, heavy-jowled, kneeling in a hotel corridor, before two pairs of shoes, a man's and a woman's, placed beside the shut door. The witty cartoon was of course a joke; but for the wider public it too literally portrayed a state of bewilderment that did not in reality exist. It belonged to the mental detective narrator of *The Sacred Fount,* not to the Henry James of the new century. In this simplification of wit Beerbohm expressed the opposite of what James was now saying" (Edel, pp. 333-34).

In the drawing James has his ear at the keyhole, while his eyes are "bulging with perception, with what Beerbohm called his 'awful

Mr. Henry James [?*c.* 1904]
Courtesy of the Ashmolean Museum, Oxford
HD 802

80

vision' of life" (Felstiner 1973, p. 149). "Your fine eyes, blurred like arc-lamps in a mist," as Max once wrote in a sonnet to James (*MV*, p. 19). 80

James's essay on D'Annunzio was first published in *The Quarterly Review* in April 1904, and Max almost certainly read it there. James's novelette *The Sacred Fount* was written in the spring of 1900, and published in 1901.

See plates 81-83.

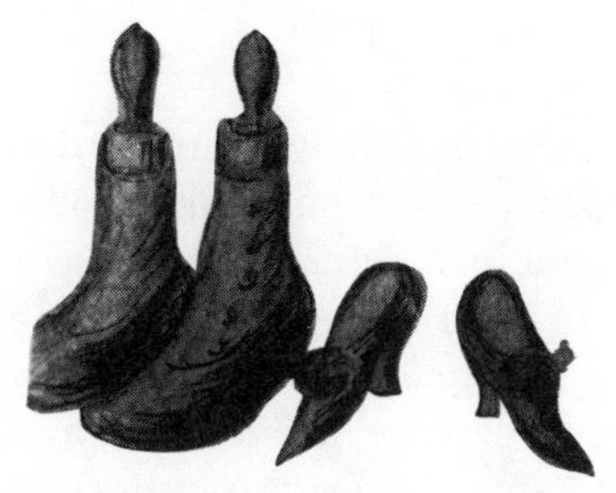

81 In 1876 James removed to England, where he lived for the rest of his life. He revisited America in 1882-83, and again in 1905. After an absence of more than twenty years, he found his native land "interesting, formidable, fearsome, and fatiguing . . . an extraordinary world, an altogether huge proposition . . . but almost cruelly charmless." His impressions of this visit are related in *The American Scene* (1907).

The drawing shows "the returned expatriate surrounded by various locals, whose reaction to him is mixed. A little girl is staring at the vast dome of his head, and exults, 'My! Ain't he cree-ative?' A Negro boy is doing a cakewalk in celebration of James's arrival; he is singing, 'We wants yer mighty badly—Yas, we *doo*!' An Indian chief is impassive but pleased: 'Hail, great white novelist! Tuniyaba—the Spinner of fine cobwebs!' A plainsman observes, 'Guess 'e ken shoot char'cter at sight!' A Negro mammy is ecstatic: 'Why, it's Masser Henry! Come to your old nurse's arms, honey!' A plump, effete Harvardian, gazing at him without enthusiasm, inquires, 'What's—the matter with—*James*?' To which a Beacon Hill hostess answers languidly, '*He's*—all—right!' A Westerner with a down-tilted stogie in his mouth looks grim and says, '*Who's*—all—right?' To which an immense plutocrat, with eyes shut, answers, '*James*!' James, not looking at anybody, lifts a deprecatory hand to still this polyphony of welcome; he is thinking (in an 'Extract from His Unspoken Thoughts'):

> . . . So that in fine, let, without further beating about the bush, me make to myself amazed acknowledgement that, but for the certificate of birth which I have—so very indubitably—*on* me, I might, in regarding, and, as it somewhat were, overseeing, *à l'oeil de voyageur,* these dear good people, find hard to swallow, or even to take by subconscious injection, the great idea that I am—oh, ever so indigenously!—one of them. . . ." (Behrman, p. 245).

The text on the drawing reads " . . . so quite indubitably. . . . " The appellation *tuniyaba* (tune-jabber?), with which the Indian chief greets the august visitor, probably echoes the criticism of those who con-

Mr. Henry James revisiting America [1905]
Courtesy of the National Gallery of Victoria, Melbourne
HD 803

81

Hail, great white novelist! Tariyaba — the Spinner of fine cobwebs!
Guess i ken shoot char'cter at sight!
Why, it's Masser Henry! Come to your old nurse's arms, honey!
What's — the matter with — James?
He's — all — right!
Who's — all — right?
James!
We wants you mighty badly. Yas, we doo!
My! Ain't he cree-ative?
Mr. Henry James revisiting America —
Extract from His Unspoken Thoughts =
....."So that in fine, let, without further beating about the bush, me make to myself amazed acknowledgment that, but for the certificate of birth which I have — so quite indubitably — on me, I might, in regarding (and, as it somewhat were, overseeing) à l'oeil de voyageur these dear good people, find hard to swallow, or even to take by subconscious injection, the great idea that I am — oh ever so indigenously! — one of them"..............
Max

demned James's later style, so brilliantly parodied in the caption to Max's drawing. Beacon Hill is a fashionable part of Boston, Massachusetts.

81

In early April 1905 Beerbohm wrote to his future wife Florence Kahn: "I have just done a rather good caricature of Henry James revisiting America. The event lends itself to comedy" (HD 803).

See plates 80, 82, 83.

82 James lived in London from 1876 to 1898. In 1898 he settled at Lamb House, Rye, Sussex, where he lived until his death.

Beerbohm first met James in 1895. "This was during James's bearded period; Max thought he looked 'like a Russian Grand Duke of the better type' and was struck by his curious 'veiled' expression. . . . 'his forehead was more than a dome, it was a whole street!'" (Cecil, pp. 154, 260). When James shaved off his beard soon after coming to Lamb House, "he looked rather like a lay Cardinal" (Hyde, p. 200).

The novelist is shown "silk-hatted and carrying an umbrella, groping through a London fog. He has his hand before his eyes, as if to be reassured by a familiar landmark" (Behrman, p. 245). The legend (not on the drawing, but in the book) parodies James's later style:

> . . . It was, therefore, not without something of a shock that he, in this to him so very congenial atmosphere, now perceived that a vision of the hand which he had, at a venture, held up within an inch or so of his eyes was, with an almost awful clarity, being adumbrated. . . .

Beerbohm's most famous parody of James is "The Mote in the Middle Distance" (*CG*, pp. 1-8; cf. SC 312). It was first published in the (London) *Saturday Review*, 8 December 1906, pp. 702-03, and contains all the turns of thought and style that can be found in James's later novels, such as *The Wings of the Dove* (1902) and *The Golden Bowl* (1904). But "The Guerdon" (*VT*, pp. 135-38), a parody of James receiving the Order of Merit, is perhaps even finer. See also Beerbohm's and Edmund Gosse's sonnet "To Henry James" and Beerbohm's "Specimen Chapter of Forthcoming Work *Half Hours with the Dialects of England*" (*MV*, pp. 19, 20-25).

Max owned copies of a number of James's books, including a first edition of *The Wings of the Dove*; a few of these were presentation copies, inscribed to him by the author (SC 121-31).

On the complex relationship between Beerbohm and James see especially Felstiner 1967. See also plates 80, 81, 83.

London in November, and Mr. Henry James in London. 1907
A Book of Caricatures (1907)
HD 804

82

83 As a young man Henry James traveled in England, France, and Italy in 1869-70. The most interesting result of this visit to Europe was the story entitled "A Passionate Pilgrim," in which he depicts the emotions of Clement Searle, a sensitive explorer of the world of his English ancestors. It was serialized in the *Atlantic Monthly* in 1871.

Beerbohm's allegorical drawing is clearly inspired by John Bunyan's *Pilgrim's Progress* (cf. Bunyan's "the City shone like the Sun," and Evangelist's advice to Christian: "Keep that light in your eye, and go up directly thereto"). It shows the aged novelist on his pilgrim's progress to the Eternal City, which, in his case of course, was Europe, the continent of his dreams. James knew Paris, Florence, Venice, and Rome very well, but the image of Rome loomed especially large for him, as it does in Beerbohm's evocation of some of Europe's most famous buildings at the end of the uphill road.

The drawing was no doubt occasioned by the subject's seventieth birthday (15 April 1913). On 11 March 1913 Beerbohm wrote to his friend Reggie Turner: "I have signed a birthday letter to Henry James—a letter to be sent to him on his seventieth birthday by a number of friends and admirers; and I have subscribed two guineas towards a birthday present to him. This present will (it is 'earnestly hoped' by the committee which is organising the sending of the letter and the buying of the present) 'take the form of a painting of Henry James himself by Mr. John Sargent.'" On his seventieth birthday James was presented with a golden bowl, in allusion to the novel of that name, and a letter from 269 friends, of whom Max was one (*LRT*, p. 222). The Sargent portrait is now in the National Portrait Gallery, London. According to Max, the famous portrait was "a dead failure, a good presentment of a butler on holiday; but no more" (Felstiner 1973, p. 155). *The Golden Bowl*, hailed by many critics as James's masterpiece, was published in 1904.

See plates 80-82.

The Old Pilgrim Comes Home. 1913
A Survey (1921)
HD 810

83

84

In 1912 Beerbohm wrote of Hall Caine (1853-1931), the English author of romantic novels with religious themes:

> Familiar to me already was that great red river of hair which, from its tiny source on the mountainous brow, spread out so quickly and flowed down so strongly and gushed at last in such torrents over the coat-collar. Viewing these rapids from a practical standpoint, I had often thought it a pity that so much force should not be utilised somehow—for turning a mill-wheel, say, or working an electrical plant. But in the course of this Sunday . . . I began to suspect that the great light of Hall Caine's eyes was indeed worked by this means; also the great and (so slight was his chest) astonishing resonance of his voice. His eyes, in their two deep caverns beneath the lower slopes of Mt. Brow, shone wondrously when he talked. His whole body seemed to quiver as though too frail for the powerful engines installed in it. I think it was this very frailty that gave to his talk, when he was in full swing, the peculiar effectiveness that it had. When a large, robust man talks loudly and well to you from the bottom of his soul, you are stirred, but not so much as when you are thus addressed by one whose body counts for so little that you seem to see as an almost physical thing the soul itself. The sight of an Atlantic liner in motion is grand; but you get a greater thrill from looking down through a hatch into the engine-room and seeing with your own eyes the monstrous forces of leaping and writhing steel there. Such a hatch—if I may say so without straining metaphor too far—was available on the surface of Hall Caine.
>
> It was the fashion to decry him. I never, thank Heaven for self-respect! went to tea-parties. But I know that at tea-parties it was always possible to raise a titter by the mere mention of Hall Caine's name. More or less it was everywhere so. And there is no denying that Hall Caine had rather brought this on himself. There had come a time when he got himself interviewed too much, photographed too much, seen too much,

Mr. Hall Caine [1899]
The Idler (London), December 1899
HD 218

84

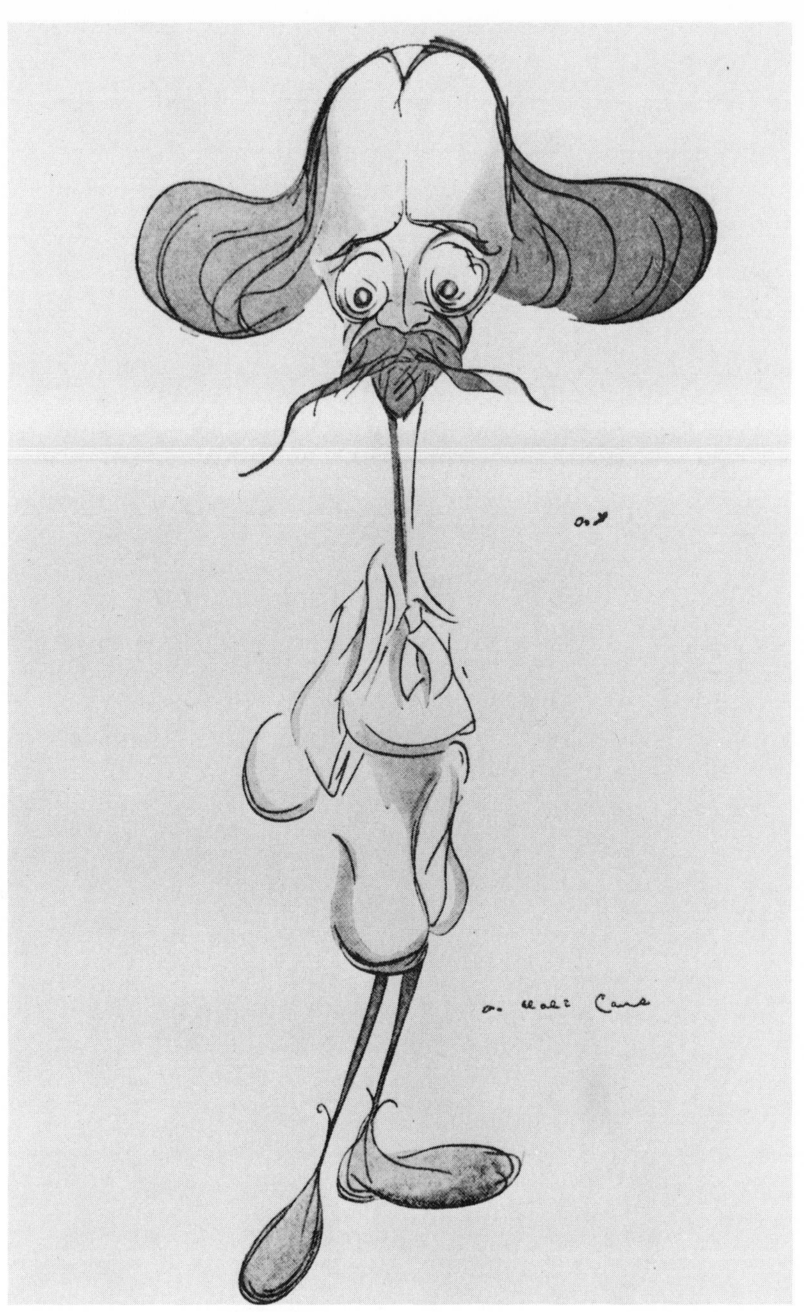

> advertised in every way too much. I think this lust for publicity 84
> may have been a result of residence with Dante Gabriel Rossetti. Conceive: a raw and excitable stripling, caught suddenly from Liverpool into still more vital London, to live incessantly apart for almost two years with a man of genius who suffered from agoraphobia in an acute form ("Nat Goodwin—and Another," *MA*, pp. 68-70; broadcast 30 May 1949).

Hall Caine was Rossetti's housemate from 1881 till the latter's death in 1882; see plates 48 and 49.

Among Hall Caine's most popular novels were *The Deemster* (1887), *The Bondman* (1890), *The Manxman* (1894), *The Christian* (1897), *The Eternal City* (1901), and *The Prodigal Son* (1904). Beerbohm wrote a withering review of *The Christian* when it came out (*The Daily Mail*, 11 August 1897, p. 4); two years later, when the book was dramatized, he referred to it as "a false, garish farrago about life in London . . . a chaotic, journalistic, pseudo-propagandist diatribe" (*MT*, p. 200).

85 Joseph Conrad (1857-1924), the English novelist, was born in Poland as Joséf Teador Konrad Korzeniowski. Because French was the second language of the educated classes in Poland, the young Conrad learned to speak it fluently while growing up. He did not begin to learn English until he was about twenty years old. After serving in the French and the British merchant marine, he became a British subject under the name of Joseph Conrad.

In his twenty years' experience of sailing the high seas, Conrad had explored the Malayan Archipelago and the coasts of many other Eastern and Western seas, but it was especially his Malayan voyages of 1887 and the Congo journey of 1890 that left their dark impact on his work.

The drawing shows the novelist, impeccably dressed and wearing a monocle, standing on the beach of some desolate coast in the Pacific, "gloating over a snake curling itself in and out of the interstices of a skull upon the seashore" (Lynch, p. 144). It is a witty commentary on Conrad's enigmatic character and his dark, fatalistic vision of life. It not only emphasizes the exotic setting of much of his work but also his sardonic, ironic concentration on the theme of death and destruction, more particularly the ruin of the isolated white man in a society which will for ever remain foreign to him—as, for instance, Almayer in *Almayer's Folly* (1895) and Willems in *An Outcast of the Islands* (1896). The snake issuing from an empty eyehole of the bleached skull symbolizes the ultimate triumph of the Malayan wilderness over the white intruder. It will be noted that the text written on the drawing is partly in French, ("Quelle charmante plage! On se fait l'illusion qu'ici on pourrait être toujours presque gai!").

Beerbohm parodied Conrad's thought and style in "The Feast" (*CG,* pp. 111-17). Its hero, Mr. Williams, and its theme are vaguely reminiscent of the hero (Willems) and theme of *An Outcast of the Islands,* certainly not one of Conrad's greater novels.

See plates 86 and 87.

Somewhere in the Pacific. 1920
A Survey (1921)
HD 359

85

MR. JOSEPH CONRAD: "What a delightful coast! One catches an illusion that one might forever be almost gay here."

86 In spite of his dark vision of life, Conrad had a tremendous power to charm. He was a spellbinding storyteller, not only in his novels and short stories, but also when he was in company. As a writer and as a storyteller he often allowed his personal experiences to coalesce imaginatively with episodes about which he had read.

The drawing shows "various sea-captains, all woe-begone, each in his individual way. Max seems to have introduced every known attitude that subtly suggests dejection. There is a depressed nigger, . . . and an old lady in a cap with a small tight bun of faded hair. Her profile not merely shows her misery, but proves it to be an irritating misery. The slightly frog-like mouth and eye, the pallor, make you feel that sadness is her occupation in life; and you want to shake her. The lamp is smoking, on the table a skull lies on a green woolly mat beneath a glass dome, and two untidy and sluttish young women lean sulkily against chairs. Mr. Conrad, very spick and span, widely grinning, is coming in at the door" (Lynch, p. 144).

The quotation in the caption is from Wordsworth's *Peter Bell,* Part First (1819), a passage which the poet omitted in later editions:

> Is it a party in a parlour?
> Cramm'd just as they on earth were cramm'd—
> Some sipping punch, some sipping tea,
> But, as you by their faces see,
> All silent and all damn'd!

The Poetical Works of William Wordsworth, II, p. 354.

See plates 85 and 87.

Mr. Conrad Again. 1920
A Survey (1921)
HD 360

86

"A party in a parlour, all silent and all damned"—and, as usual, Mr. Joseph Conrad intruding.

87 One of a series of drawings entitled "The Old and the Young Self," published in *Observations*; see plate 26.

The language used by the novelist's Young Self is not actually Polish, but a gibberish invented by Max, though the first two words sound like Polish, and some of the others suggest the rich consonantal quality of that language. Conrad obtained his Master Mariner's certificate in 1886. The words "Mais oui, mon enfant" remind one of Conrad's habit of ironically punctuating his narratives with French phrases; the habit may have been due to his fluency in French, or to his reading of de Maupassant, whose work was one of the major formative influences on his art.

John Galsworthy once described Conrad as "a dark-haired man, short but extemely graceful in his nervous gestures, with brilliant eyes, now narrowed and penetrating, now soft and warm, with a manner alert yet caressing, whose speech was ingratiating, guarded and brusque by turn. I had never seen before a man so masculinely keen yet so femininely sensitive." Ford Madox Ford said that "when you had really secured his attention he would insert a monocle into his right eye and scrutinize your face as a watchmaker looks into the works of a watch" (Warner, pp. 15-16).

When, in 1905, the Stage Society, London, produced Conrad's *One Day More,* a dramatization of one of his short stories, Beerbohm hailed him as a master of fiction "who ought to be coaxed into writing plays;" this little one-act play was "terrible and haunting" and "a powerful tragedy" (*AT*, pp. 384-87).

See plates 85 and 86.

The Old and the Young Self: Joseph Conrad. 1924
Observations (1925)
HD 362

87

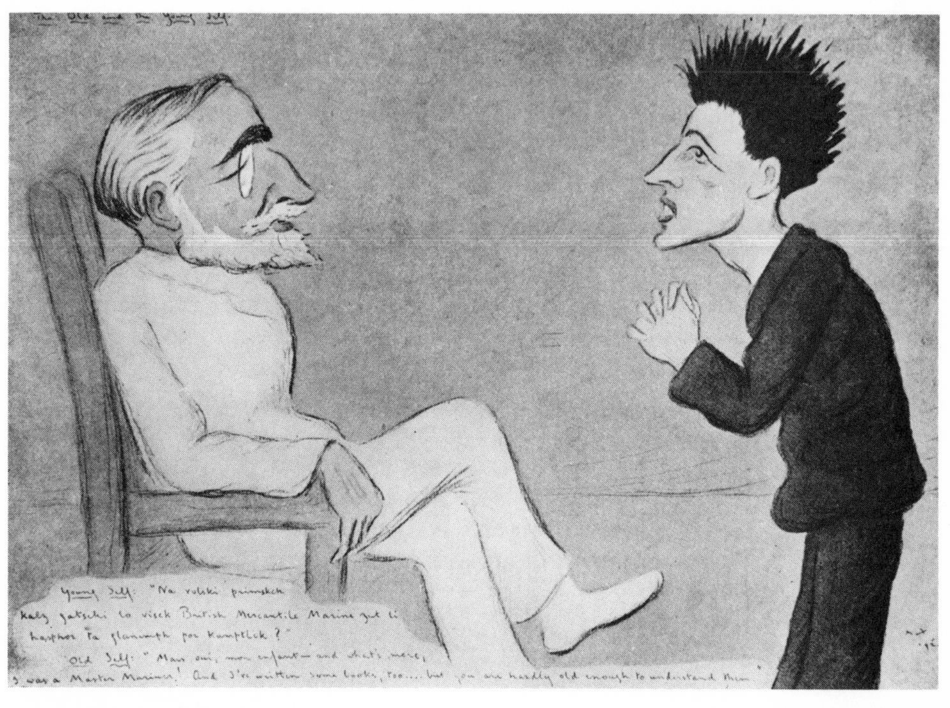

YOUNG SELF: "Na volski primskch kalz gatscki lo visck British Mercantile Marine zut li hasphor ta glanimph por kumptlck?"

OLD SELF: "Mais oui, mon enfant—and what's more, I was a Master Mariner! And I've written some books, too . . . but you are hardly old enough to understand them."

88 After his father's death in 1870, George Augustus Moore (1852-1933), the Irish novelist and playwright, went to Paris, where he mixed with the poets and artists for some ten years and made half-hearted attempts to study painting.

The following impression is from Beerbohm's essay "George Moore," written in 1913, and broadcast on 6 October 1950:

> His Parisianism, grafted upon an imperishable brogue, gave to his utterance a very curious charm. Aided by his face and his gesture, this charm was irresistible. I say his 'gesture' advisedly; for he had but one. The finger-tips of his vague, small, inert, white hand continually approached his mouth and, rising thence, described an arc in the air—a sort of invisible suspension-bridge for the passage of his i-de-a to us. His face, too, while he talked, had but one expression—a faintly-illumined blank. Usually, when even the most phlegmatic of men is talking, you shall detect changes of expression. In Moore you never could. Usually the features of the most vivacious man's face retain the form that Nature assigned to them. But in Moore's face, immutable though the expression was, by some physical miracle the features were perpetually remoulding themselves. It was not merely that the chin receded and progressed, nor merely that the oval cheeks went rippling in capricious hollows and knolls: the contours of nose and brow, they too, had their vicissitudes. You think I exaggerate? Well, I myself, with Moore there before me, did sometimes doubt the evidence of my own eyes. It was possible that my eyes had been deceived. But the point then is that no face save Moore's ever deceived them in just this way (*MA*, pp. 76-77).

Moore's principal works are *A Modern Lover* (1883), *A Drama in Muslin* (1886), *Confessions of a Young Man* (1888), *Esther Waters* (1894), *Evelyn Innes* (1898), *Sister Teresa* (1901), *Memoirs of My Dead Life* (1906), the trilogy *Hail and Farewell: Ave* (1911), *Salve* (1912), *Vale* (1914), *The Brook Kerith: A Syrian Story* (1916), *Hēloïse and Abēlard* (1921).

In the Robert H. Taylor Collection in the Princeton University

Mr. George Moore [1896]
Caricatures of Twenty-Five Gentlemen (1896)
HD 1044

88

Library there is a copy of Max's *Caricatures of Twenty-Five Gentlemen* 88
(1896) in which the artist, twenty-four years after publication, has redrawn Moore on the blank page facing the caricature. Beerbohm's annotation reads: "Time has been kind to George Moore. Fate said, 'This child, when he comes to man's estate, shall have a complexion like inferior white wax, and hair like bad flax. And he shall write very badly.' Time, twenty years later, said, 'This gifted young man shall learn to write grammatically and well before he is quite old. And when he is quite old he shall have very pretty silver hair, and a complexion like a baby's.' An unusual case. Everything about G. M. is unusual" (Felstiner 1972, fig. 12). To understand this passage, one should remember Oscar Wilde's remark that Moore took seven years to discover grammar, that he then discovered the paragraph, and so on, shouting his discoveries from the housetop as he went along (Hone, pp. 25, 97).

Moore felt that Max had caricatured him out of all human resemblance (Hart-Davis lists as many as nineteen major Beerbohm caricatures of Moore, Nos. 1044-62); but as Moore aged, "he . . . grew to look like the person Beerbohm had been drawing" (Felstiner 1972, pp. 80-81).

See plates 32, 33, 51, 89-91.

89 "There always was an illusory look about him—the diaphanous, vaporous, wan look of an illusion conjured up for us, perhaps by means of mirrors and by a dishonourable spiritualist. There was something blurred about him; his outlines seemed to merge into the air around him. He never seemed to enter or leave a room. Rather did he appear there, and in due time fade thence. It was always difficult to say at what moment he appeared: one had but become aware of his presence, which was always delightful, and later one found oneself missing him: he had gone. . . . He sat rather on the edge of his chair, his knees together, his hands hanging limp on either side of him. Limply there hung over his brow a copious wisp of blond hair, which wavered as he turned the long white oval of his face from one speaker to another. He sat wide-eyed, gaping, listening—no, one would not have said 'listening' but hearing: it did not seem that his ears were sending in any reports to his brain. It would be an under-statement to say that his face was as a mask which revealed nothing. His face was as a mask of gauze through which Nothing was quite clearly visible. And then, all of a sudden, there would appear—Something. There came a gleam from within the pale-blue eyes, and a sort of ripple passed up over the modelling of the flaccid cheeks; the chin suddenly receded a little further, and—*Voilà Moore qui parle! Silence, la compagnie! Moore parle*" ("George Moore," *MA*, pp. 74, 76).

See plates 32, 33, 51, 88, 90, 91.

George Moore [n. d.]
Courtesy of the Ashmolean Museum, Oxford
HD 1058

89

90 Once, when Moore was writing his novel *Evelyn Innes,* he asked Arthur Symons: "Does anyone here know an opera singer? I am writing a story about an opera singer. I must have a model. What can you *do* without a model. To write a book about an opera singer without knowing one, and even sleeping with her, is to expose oneself to defeat" (Hone, p. 208).

From 1911 until the end of his life Moore lived at 121 Ebury Street, near Chelsea. In *His Fatal Beauty; or The Moore of Chelsea,* a play by E. V. Lucas, acted at the Chelsea Palace, 20 March 1917, and privately printed by Clement Shorter (25 copies only) that same year, Moore is made to say: "Yes, this is Chelsea and I am its most famous inhabitant." To which Sir Peter Lely replies: "Aye, and the handsomest" (p. 12).

Beerbohm was amused by Moore's desire to be regarded as a lady killer. The following lines were written by him in his copy of the 1921 edition of Moore's *Memoirs of My Dead Life*:

Vague Lyric by G. M.

I met Musette
In the water-closet—
Or if it wasn't there, where *was* it?
And let me see:
Was it not Mimi
That made such passionate love to me
In the W.C.?
Which *was* it?

MV, p. 113.

When this caricature was published, Max changed the word "Re-appearance", which occurs on the drawing, to "Rentrée" in the letterpress accompanying it in *Fifty Caricatures.* The printed text also has "poor" instead of "pore."

Cf. Beerbohm's "Elegy on Any Lady by George Moore" (*MV,* p. 47), and plates 32, 33, 51, 88, 89, 91.

Rentrée of Mr. George Moore into Chelsea. 1909
Fifty Caricatures (1913)
HD 1050

ARTIST'S MODEL: "Ought to be ashamed o' yerself—coming an' taking the bread out o' us poor girls' mouths."

91 One of a series of drawings entitled "The Old and the Young Self," published in *Observations*; see plate 26. The drawing shows "the young George Moore, rubbery, amorphous, [standing] obeisantly, silk hat in hand, before the old George, more rubbery still but sitting" (Behrman, p. 254). The picture on the wall is an evocation of the young Moore with two admiring ladies.

When he lived in Paris, Moore became acquainted with the French impressionist painters Édouard Manet (1832-83) and Edgar Degas (1834-1917) and their circle of friends. There is a drawing of Moore as a young man in Paris by Manet. In *His Fatal Beauty; or The Moore of Chelsea* by E. V. Lucas (see note to plate 90) Moore is made to say: "I go back into the past only as far as Manet" (p. 13). The other references in the caption are to Richard Wagner (1813-83), the German composer whose music and letters to Mathilde Wesendonk Moore admired, and to Honoré de Balzac (1799-1850), "the father of the modern novel," on whom Moore read a paper in 1910.

Beerbohm owned copies of the first editions of two of Moore's books, *Reminiscences of the Impressionist Painters* (1906), and *Hail and Farewell* (3 vols., 1911, 1912, 1914), both with autograph presentation inscriptions by the author, and also a copy of the 1921 edition of *Memoirs of My Dead Life* (SC 157-59).

Max parodied Moore's thought and style in "Dickens" (*CG*, pp. 159-66). For Beerbohm on Moore see *AT*, pp. 58-61, and *MT*, pp. 104-09. See also plates 32, 33, 51, 88-90.

The Old and the Young Self: Mr. George Moore. 1924
Observations (1925)
HD 1056

91

Young Self: "And have there been any painters since Manet?"
Old Self: "None."
Young Self: "Have there been any composers since Wagner?"
Old Self: "None."
Young Self: "Any novelists since Balzac?"
Old Self: "One."

92 From 1896 to 1900 Maurice Henry Hewlett (1861-1923), the English novelist, poet, and essayist, was Keeper of Land Revenue Records and Enrolments. He was of an old English family who owned land in the borders of Somerset and Dorset for many centuries. In fact, there is a person by the name of Hewlett mentioned in the Domesday Book of Somerset as holding land there.

Hewlett's first novel *The Forest Lovers* (1898) was an immediate success, and is still popular with vast sections of the reading public. But his best work is his epic poem *The Song of the Plow,* published in 1916. Hewlett was a lover of the country, and the poems of his last years are passionate expressions of his belief in the English peasantry as the only hope for England.

Beerbohm parodied Hewlett's prose style in "Fond Hearts Askew" (*CG,* pp. 149-57). On 10 March 1906 he reviewed *The Youngest of the Angels,* a dramatization of a scene in Hewlett's *The Fool Errant* (*LT,* pp. 235-39). In his Rede Lecture, 1943, he said of Hewlett: "I have always regretted that Maurice Hewlett, one of the lights of the 'nineties and of later years, was not a humourist and wished to illude us with his tales; for his preciosity was fatal to his wish. Besides, it was a robust preciosity; and that is unnatural, is a contradiction in terms" (*LS,* p. 23).

Mr. Maurice Hewlett being photographed. 1921
A Survey (1921)
HD 749

92

93 The drawing represents Robert Smythe Hichens (1864-1950), author of *The Green Carnation* (1894) and of such immensely popular novels as *The Garden of Allah* (1904), with great affability, stirring his tea.

"Some time in the summer of 1894 [Reggie Turner] introduced Max to a young man called Robert Hichens, a music critic and journalist and destined later to become a successful popular novelist. He was a plump, genial-looking youth, of simple straightforward manners, who enjoyed a good game of golf and a good dinner after it. He was also quick and clever and immediately appreciated Max. Max—who never minded simplicity and enjoyed being appreciated as much as most people—responded."

"Early in their acquaintance Hichens showed Max a book he had written called *The Green Carnation*. It was a skit on aestheticism and its chief characters were drawn from Oscar Wilde and Alfred Douglas, who he had met abroad. Max found it very entertaining and went through it carefully with the author. It appeared in September and made a sensation—also a scandal. For it touched on what had become a scandalous topic. The clouds were gathering above Oscar's head and he was rapidly acquiring an extremely sinister reputation, mainly on account of his association with Alfred Douglas" (Cecil, pp. 107, 108).

On 18 November 1937 Beerbohm wrote to his friend Turner that he had devoured the Hichens books he had sent him, adding: "With what a little difference would Crotchet be a really great novelist!" (*LRT*, p. 280; as a music critic Hichens had written articles under the name of Crotchet). In *Yesterday: The Autobiography of Robert Hichens* (1947) Hichens refers to Max Beerbohm on pp. 66, 85-86, 89.

R. S. Hichens Esq [1896]
Caricatures of Twenty-Five Gentlemen (1896)
HD 750

93

R S Hichens Esq

94 Before 1907, the date of the drawing, Herbert George Wells (1866-1946), the English novelist, journalist, sociologist, and popular historian, had already written on such subjects as "Popularising Science" (*Nature*, 26 July 1894), "Human Evolution an Artificial Process" (*Fortnightly Review*, October 1896), *Anticipations of the Reaction of Mechanical and Scientific Progress upon Human Life* (1902), *The Discovery of the Future* (1902), "'State Babies' and 'A Woman's Day in Utopia'"(*Daily Mail*, 20 April and 7 June 1905), *A Modern Utopia* (1905), and *Socialism and the Family* (1906).

In this drawing Max gives us an unappetizing picture of the future as imagined by the progressive Wells. Wells, "all head and eyes, is talking to himself, zoning Utopia, but his remarks are being overheard by an unattractive female with glasses, holding a mathematical symbol in one hand and a baby in the other. The baby is wearing glasses, too, and is evidently to be consigned to a day nursery in Utopia, where he, or she, will be given a number" (Behrman, p. 237).

During a weekend at Faringdon with Lord Berners in December 1946, Beerbohm spoke "with loving veneration of Thomas Hardy's character; his noble simplicity, his beautiful modesty about his own work. With less approval he spoke about H. G. Wells. His interlocutor thought that this was because Max identified Wells with the scientific advances now manifesting themselves in the disagreeable guise of air warfare. 'You mean,' he suggested, 'that he is partly responsible for our present ills.' 'He was responsible for himself,' said Max crisply, 'and that was one of the worst of them. He was at once a man of real genius and a mean bounder. It is a rare combination.' As Max spoke, his voice changed, a new and incisive severity came into his tones. Suddenly he sounded formidable" (Cecil, p. 463).

See Beerbohm's lines "In a copy of More's (or Shaw's or Wells's or Plato's or anybody's) *Utopia*" (*MV*, p. 54), and also plates 95 and 97.

A Book of Caricatures (1907)
HD 1756

94

Mr. H. G. Wells, prophet and idealist, conjuring up the darling Future.
1907

95 One of a series of drawings entitled "The Old and the Young Self," published in *Observations*; see plate 26.

In the drawing the young self of Wells alludes briefly to his zoological studies. As a young man he had written a *Text-Book of Biology* (1893). In his scientific romances, such as *The Time Machine* (1895), *The Invisible Man* (1897), *The War of the Worlds* (1898), *The First Men in the Moon* (1901), and in books like *Anticipations* (1901), he had dealt with the possible impact of science on the future of man. It was not until his seventy-sixth year that he sought and obtained the degree of Doctor of Science of the University of London. Of his doctoral dissertation, *A Thesis on the Quality of Illusion in the Continuity of the Individual Life in the Higher Metazoa, with particular reference to the species Homo Sapiens,* only a few copies were printed for private distribution in 1942. An abridgment of it was published in *Nature,* 1 April 1944, and issued separately that same year under the title *The Illusion of Personality.* The most popular of all of Wells's books, *The Outline of History,* appeared in 1919.

Beerbohm parodied Wells's thought and style in "The Defossilized Plum-Pudding," a story of a man who defossilizes a cannon-ball and makes it into a Christmas pudding (*The Saturday Review,* Christmas Supplement, 1896). His other parody of Wells, "Perkins and Mankind" (*CG*, pp. 29-43), is an expansion of "General Cessation Day," published in *The Saturday Review* of 29 December 1906. The term "microglamaphoid" in the caption of the drawing is a nonce-word coined by Max.

See plates 94 and 97.

The Old and the Young Self: Mr. H. G. Wells. 1924
Observations (1925)
HD 1758

95

Young Self: "Did you ever manage to articulate the bones of that microglamaphoid lizard?"

Old Self: "I'm not sure. But I've articulated the whole past of mankind on this planet—and the whole future too. I don't think you know very much about the past, do you? It's all perfectly beastly, believe me. But the future's going to be all perfectly splendid . . . after a bit. And I must say I find the present very jolly."

96 In 1910 Arnold Bennett (1867-1931), the English novelist and playwright, published his novel *Clayhanger,* the first volume of an ambitious trilogy. Its sequel was *Hilda Lessways* (1911), but the concluding volume, *These Twain,* did not appear until 1916.

The drawing represents Bennett being chided by the heroine of *Hilda Lessways* for delaying the last volume of his trilogy; the respectable Edwin Clayhanger dismally waits behind Hilda. The title refers to Bennett's *Milestones,* a play in three acts, written in collaboration with Edward Knoblock; this play had been a great success on the London stage in 1912, a year before this drawing was made. At Beerbohm's second Leicester Galleries, London, exhibition, which opened on 11 April 1913, the drawing was bought by Bennett himself.

At the beginning of *Hilda Lessways* it is stated that the heroine of the book is "within a few weeks of twenty-one." The drawing was made and published in 1913. To a reader in that year Hilda would therefore have been "born" in 1892, which is exactly the date engraved on the milestone.

When Beerbohm read *Clayhanger* in 1910, he thought it "rather a pale reflex of the *Old Wives* [i.e., Bennett's *The Old Wives' Tale*], but interesting." Four years later he wrote to Reggie Turner that Henry James once said that *Hilda Lessways* was "like the slow squeezing-out of a big, dirty sponge," though he would not perhaps put it in writing (*LRT*, pp. 193, 232).

Beerbohm parodied Bennett's thought and style in "Scruts" (*CG*, pp. 75-89). The word was invented by Max for the broken pieces of pottery which, according to him, the inhabitants of the Five Towns, which figure prominently in Bennett's novels, mix into their Christmas puddings instead of sixpences. Max owned a copy of the 1909 edition of *The Old Wives' Tale* (SC 4).

See plates 33, 97, 98.

A Milestone. 1913

Courtesy of the Robert H. Taylor Collection, Princeton, N. J.

HD 132

96

HILDA LESSWAYS (TO THE AUTHOR OF HER BEING): "Now then, Mister Bennett, how much longer d'you mean to keep me and Clayhanger standing about here? I never heard of such goings on."

97 In October 1922, at very short notice, H. G. Wells (1866-1946) was asked, and agreed, to stand as Labour candidate for the University of London constituency. His original election address was printed that same year by St. Clements Press, London, but owing to Post Office disqualification the pamphlet *The World, its Debts, and the Rich Men* (London: St. Clements Press, 1922) was substituted as an emergency election address. Wells's two electoral letters for the General Election of 1923 were printed by the Pelican Press that same year. His candidature was unsuccessful.

Bennett and Wells were close friends. Bennett admired Wells's genius, and Wells considered Bennett the best friend he had ever had. Max must have known that, in 1912, Wells had dedicated his novel *Marriage* "fraternally to Arnold Bennett." Bennett's tufted forelock, "curling like votive smoke and balancing, by design, the deep indented chin," had become a true *panache,* by which one could pick him out at once in a crowd (Pound, pp. 7, 328).

Max Beerbohm once said of Bennett: "Arnold was a card, all right, but without guile. At his birth, his good fairy must have promised, 'I will make him ill-favored, crude, egotistical, but I will give him a stutter that will draw people to him, make them sympathetic to him, and listen to him'" (Behrman, p. 248).

To understand this drawing it should be remembered that Bennett made a lot of money from his novels: they were bestsellers. Up to 1916 his *Clayhanger,* published in 1910, had sold 37,000 copies, *Hilda Lessways* (1911) 34,000, *The Card* (1911) 53,000, and *These Twain* (1916) 34,000. However, "the money-making prowess of Arnold Bennett is not likely to have contributed much to his wider reputation, though his boasted half-a-crown-a-word rate of payment from editors gained him notoriety, not to say envy, in Fleet Street" (Pound, p. 5).

The words "(*December, 1922.*)" do not appear on the drawing.

See plates 33, 94-96, 98.

Mr. H. G. Wells "fraternally" urging Mr. Arnold Bennett to try too. (*December, 1922.*). 1922

Courtesy of the Ashmolean Museum, Oxford

HD 134

97

Mr. Bennett: "Parliament, eh? Well, get 'em to raise the screw to forty-thou', and perhaps I'll think of it."

98 One of a series of drawings entitled "The Old and the Young Self," published in *Observations*; see plate 26.

In this caricature Arnold Bennett's Old Self, "in white tie, oozing affluence, immense of girth, toothy, a figure of dishevelled elegance, befobbed and wearing a pleated shirt, his pudgy hands clutching his white waistcoat, and his face bearing an expression of not entirely convinced complacency, is addressing his Young Self, a scrawny, stubborn yokel from Staffordshire" (Behrman, p. 253).

In 1901 Bennett wrote of his future to a friend: "Although I am thirty-three and have not made a name, I infallibly know that I *shall* make a name and that soon. But I should like to be a legend." Referring to *The Old Wives' Tale,* he wrote in 1907: "I calculated that it would be 200,000 words long (which it exactly proved to be)" (Pound, p. 181). Passages like these abound in his journals and letters. As a result of his systematic industry Bennett certainly succeeded in making a name, though he has not become a legend.

Beerbohm admired Bennett's talent enormously. *The Old Wives' Tale* (1908) deeply impressed him: it was a great novel, though written without charm or distinction. But its author was "a true seer and interpreter of life, focussing his vision not on any one little phase, but on the whole range of things." Bennett's other books keenly disappointed Max: they were pot-boilers, though he found his play *What the Public Wants* (1909) "one of the best comedies of our time" (*LT*, pp. 455, 456). As for Bennett himself, he once described Beerbohm's *Yet Again* as "an absolute masterpiece" (*Journals,* I, p. 337, n. 2).

See plates 33, 96, 97.

The Old and the Young Self: Mr. Arnold Bennett. 1924

Courtesy of the Humanities Research Center, The University of Texas at Austin

HD 135

98

OLD SELF: "All gone according to plan, you see."
YOUNG SELF: "*My* plan, you know."

99 "Stephen Hudson" was the pseudonym of the English novelist Sydney Schiff (1868-1944). He and his wife Violet were wealthy patrons of authors and artists. On their visits to Paris they met Marcel Proust, whose correspondence with them began in April 1919 and continued until September 1922, two months before Proust's death. (The letters are now in the British Library.) In 1931 Schiff published an English translation of Proust's *Le Temps Retrouvé*, one of the volumes of *À la Recherche du Temps Perdu*, under the title *Time Regained*. Schiff's novel *A True Story* has been reprinted several times. Beerbohm owned a presentation copy of a 1930 edition of it, with a long autograph inscription by the author on the fly-leaf, in the form of a letter. He also owned copies of seven other books by Sydney Schiff, most of them with presentation inscriptions by the author (SC 195).

During the first years of the Second World War, the Beerbohms lived in a little Tudor house, Abinger Manor Cottage, at Abinger Common, near Dorking, Surrey. It had been lent them by their friend Sydney Schiff, whose wife Violet was a sister of the novelist Ada Leverson (1862-1933), Oscar Wilde's "Sphinx." Beerbohm had known her since she had published an interview with him in *The Sketch* (London), 2 January 1895, p. 439; she became one of Beerbohm's close correspondents (Riewald 1953, p. 305, No. 590a).

"Stephen Hudson." 1925
Observations (1925)
HD 1385

99

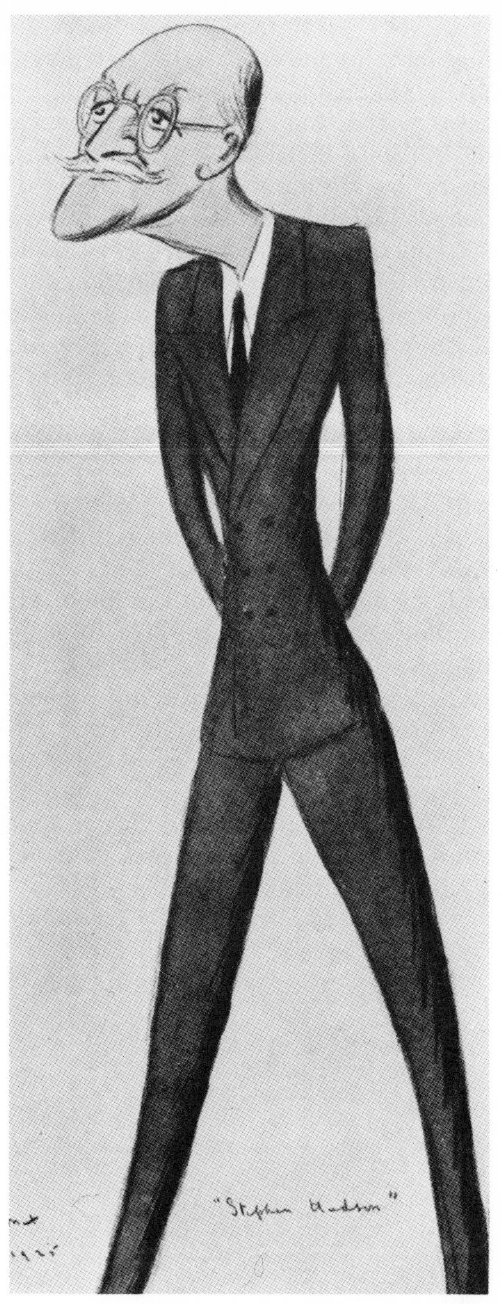

100

For many years Norman Douglas (1868-1952), the English novelist and essayist, lived on the island of Capri in the bay of Naples. His first book, *Siren Land* (1911), was a complete failure, but it was reprinted in 1923, the year in which Max drew this caricature, and has since been widely read. Douglas's first popular success was *South Wind* (1917), which was reprinted eighteen times between its publication and 1935. This satirical novel is set in the Mediterranean island of Nepenthe (Capri). The island is visited by the narrow-minded Anglican bishop of Bampopo, who is profoundly influenced by his brief stay in the Mediterranean. Among the characters he meets are an American "Duchess" hovering on the brink of conversion to Roman Catholicism, and Don Francesco, a popular ecclesiastic, "worldly wise, indolent, good-natured," an unrivaled preacher, and "a thoroughgoing pagan."

A *gourmet* and a lover of wine, Norman Douglas's philosophy of life was Epicurean. He was very outspoken in his criticism of Christianity, especially of Roman Catholicism. He once said that he had taken a vow never to enter a church.

In a recent (1969) broadcast talk Sir Compton Mackenzie recalled his friendship with Norman Douglas in these words: "To sit with him on a *terrazza* in the sweet South, thatched with broom against the fierce noonday sun, between us a flask of red or white wine, and talk the hours away was, for me, like sitting with Horace at his Sabine farm. *Nunc vino pellite curas.* Now banish with wine all cares. *Carpe diem.* Gather today, and put not the smallest faith in tomorrow."

As far as I know, there is no such wine as Bombarolina. Max probably invented the word to emphasize, by its sound, the persistent force of Douglas's argument. Max's own favorite wine was Bardolino.

Beerbohm owned a copy of *Alone* (1921), one of Norman Douglas's Italian travel books (SC 58).

Things New and Old (1923)
HD 444

100

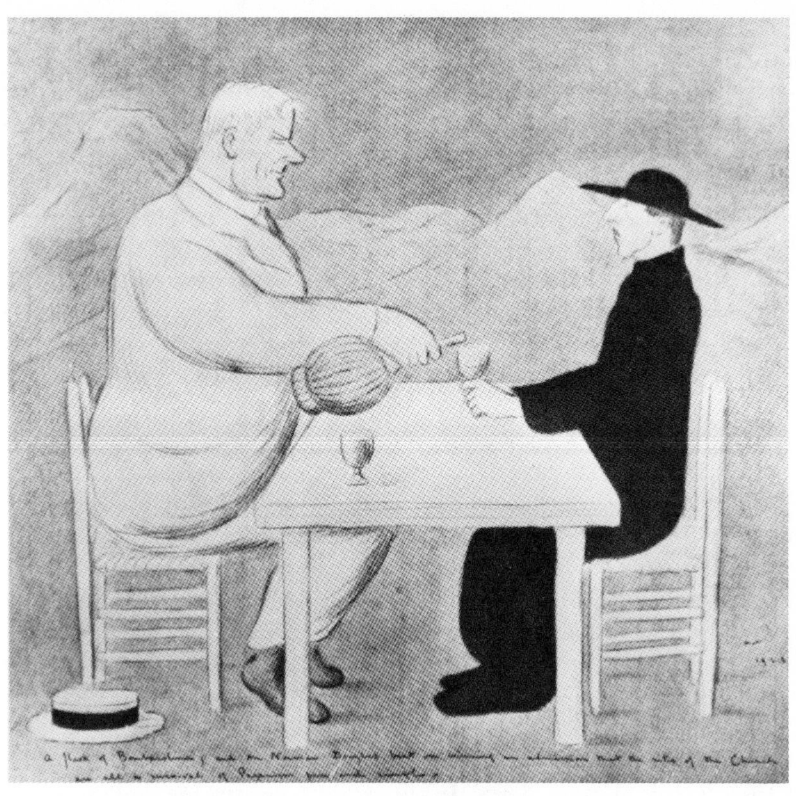

A Flask of Bombarolina; and Mr. Norman Douglas bent on winning an admission that the rites of the Church are all a survival of Paganism pure and simple. 1923

101 Reginald ("Reggie") Turner (1869-1938), journalist, controversial wit, and author of a dozen unsuccessful novels, was among Beerbohm's closest friends. Beerbohm and Turner carried on a steady correspondence from 1891 until Turner's death; Beerbohm's letters to Turner were published by Sir Rupert Hart-Davis in 1964 (*LRT*). In later years Beerbohm said that he was glad that his letters to other people were not so asinine as those to Reggie had been (Cecil, p. 79). Max did at least fourteen caricatures of his friend (HD 1681A-88A).

In his essay "Laughter" (*AEN*, pp. 291-308) Max introduces Reggie as Comus, the "incomparable laughter-giver." Beerbohm himself appears, thinly disguised as Hans Branders, in Turner's novel *Davray's Affairs*. Turner's sympathetic analysis of Hans's character probably suggested to Max the caption of this caricature, which was done in 1907, a year after Turner's book was published.

Turner was "fantastically ugly, with a nut-shaped head, blubbery lips and a huge snout-like nose . . . he was continually winking and blinking. But he had intelligence and sensibility, a warm, delicate, generous nature, and an extraordinary gift of humour. Some expert judges, including Max himself and Mr. Somerset Maugham, have judged him to be the most amusing man they ever met in their lives" (Cecil, p. 53).

When Max showed him this caricature, S.N. Behrman reacted as follows: "The great promontory of Reginald Turner's nose suddenly jutted before us. I have never seen such a nose; . . . 'How did your friend Turner feel about *that*?' I asked. 'Oh, well, you know,' said Max, 'when you exaggerate as much as that, there can be no offense in it'" (Behrman, p. 237).

Beerbohm reviewed a performance of Turner's *Prince Pierrot* on 25 July 1903 (*MT*, pp. 588-91). Turner's collection of Beerbohm caricatures, comprising about thirty items, was included in the sale of his books held by Sotheby, London, on 24-25 July 1939. The collection was dispersed.

See also Max's "Rondeau d'Admonition," *MV*, p. 6, and SC 231.

A Psychologist: Mr. Reginald Turner. 1907
A Book of Caricatures (1907)
HD 1683

101

102 One of a series of drawings entitled "The Old and the Young Self," published in *Observations*; see plate 26.

The caption on the drawing reads: *The Old and the Young Self*—and "The Puppet Show of Memory." Maurice Baring (1874-1945), the English novelist, poet, and dramatist, was the author of a volume of reminiscences down to the year 1914, *The Puppet Show of Memory* (1922). In this book his reception into the Roman Catholic Church in 1909 is referred to in a single sentence as "the only action in my life which I am quite certain I have never regretted."

Of Baring's *The Grey Stocking*, performed in London in 1908, Beerbohm wrote that it was a play "where nothing comes of anything, and where no one is an outwardly exciting person." According to him, Baring had merely proved that he was an "adramatist" (*AT*, pp. 512-16).

Beerbohm parodied Baring's thought and style in "All Roads—" (*CG*, 1950 edition, pp. 55-65). In a postscript to this edition Beerbohm refers to Baring as "my old friend, the brilliant, the greatly gifted Maurice Baring." About the parody itself Baring wrote to Beerbohm: "Its only fault is that it is so much better than anything I could have done myself, and reveals a higher intelligence and a better craftsman" (Felstiner 1973, p. 162).

Max owned a copy of Baring's novel *Cat's Cradle* (1925) (SC 4).

The Old and the Young Self: Mr. Maurice Baring. 1924
Observations (1925)
HD 90

102

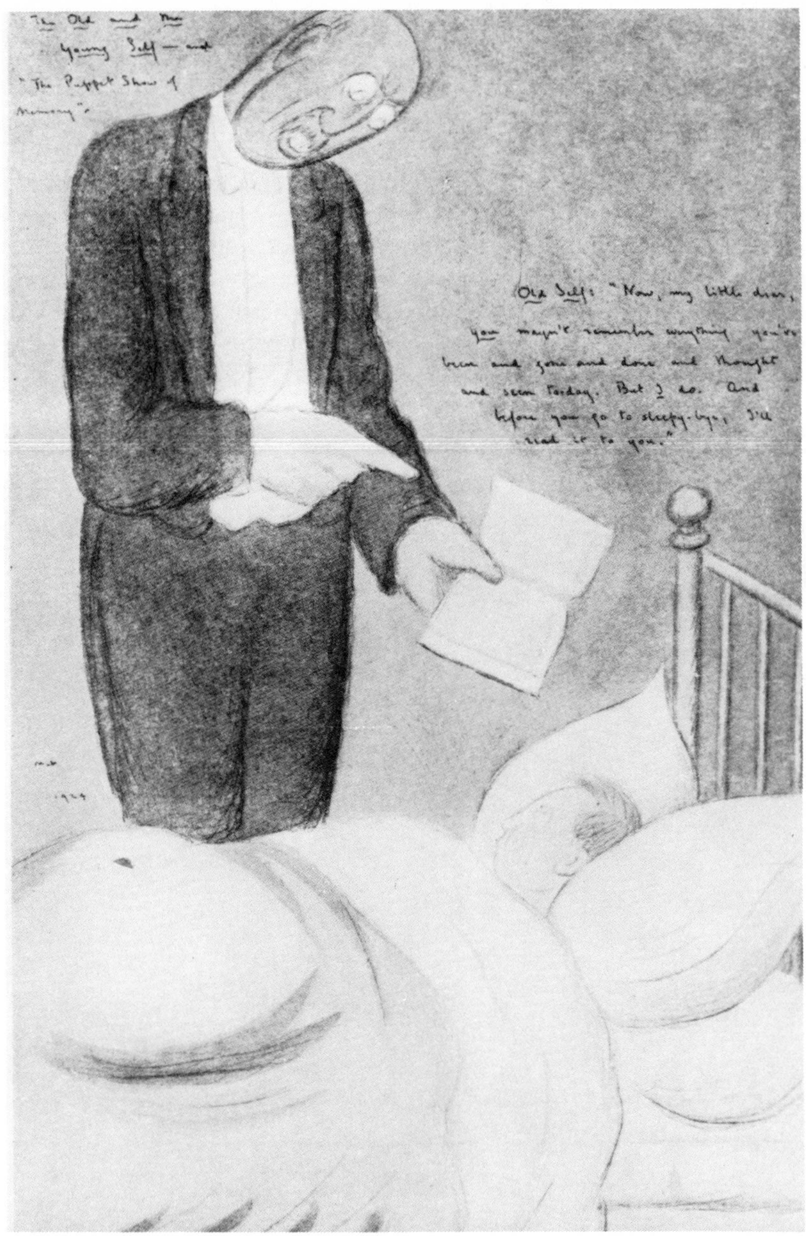

Old Self: "Now, my little dear, *you* mayn't remember everything you've been and gone and done and thought and seen to-day. But *I* do. And before you go to sleepy-bye, I'll read it to you."

103 Arthur Stuart Menteth Hutchinson (1879-1971), the romantic and sentimental English novelist, has been described as shy to the verge of timidity, with extreme modesty, amounting almost to an inferiority complex. In 1921 he achieved a resounding success with his novel *If Winter Comes.* In the drawing, made two years after the publication of this book, success is allegorically represented by a huge, forbidding woman, holding a pineapple. Though the book was parodied at once, it was reprinted several times, and even made into a play in 1928. In spite of this success, Hutchinson went on publishing at fairly wide intervals, keeping himself as much out of the limelight as possible. In 1958 he published his recollections of his early life under the title *Bring Back the Days.*

Mr. A. S. M. Hutchinson, much embarrassed. 1923
Things New and Old (1923)
HD 779

103

Success! So this was she! In his youth he had often dreamed of her; but he had not imagined her quite like this. This was she! Success!

104 Aldous Leonard Huxley (1894-1963), the English novelist, essayist, and poet, belonged to a distinguished family. He was the son of Leonard Huxley, editor of the *Cornhill Magazine*, and grandson of the illustrious scientist Thomas Henry Huxley; Sir Julian Huxley, the biologist and writer, is his brother.

By 1923, the year in which the drawing was made, Aldous Huxley had published three collections of poems, two collections of short stories, one book of notes and essays, and two novels, *Crome Yellow* (1921) and *Antic Hay* (1923). Beerbohm owned a 1922 copy of *Crome Yellow* and a copy of *Mortal Coils* (1922), a collection of short stories (SC 4 and 118); the latter contains about forty sketch-portraits, mostly profiles, of Norman Douglas, some of a female impersonator (? Vesta Tilley), etc., by Max Beerbohm, drawn in pencil on sixteen blank pages.

At the age of sixteen Huxley was threatened by near or total blindness. An old pupil remembers him as his schoolmaster at Eton: "... that long, thin body with a face that was far younger than most of our masters' and yet seemed somehow ageless, and, usually hidden by an infinite variety of spectacles, eyes that were almost sightless and yet almost uncomfortably observant" (*Aldous Huxley, 1894-1963,* p. 27). More recently Lord David Cecil described him as "a very distinguished, very long, tall, pale piece of macaroni" (*The Listener,* 24 December 1970, p. 868). Max's drawing emphasizes the author's weak vision, but also his abnormal height.

Mr. Aldous Huxley. 1923
Things New and Old (1923)
HD 780

104

Bibliographical Note

Fifty-five of the drawings in this book have been reproduced from the collections of caricatures published by Max Beerbohm, as follows:

Caricatures of Twenty-Five Gentlemen. With an Introduction by L. Raven-Hill. London: Leonard Smithers, 1896

Twenty-five numbered wood engravings, printed on rectos only; each plate preceded by a leaf with descriptive letterpress printed on recto.

The Poets' Corner. London: William Heinemann, 1904.

Twenty unnumbered caricatures, lithographed in color on rectos only, with descriptive letterpress at bottom.

The drawings were shown at the Carfax Gallery, London, May 1904; see *Caricatures by Max Beerbohm.* London: Carfax & Co., 1904.

A Book of Caricatures. London: Methuen & Co. [1907].

Frontispiece in color; forty-eight caricatures in halftone, pasted on rectos of white cardboard mounts, each preceded by a tissue guard sheet with printed roman numeral and title of caricature in facsimile of the artist's handwriting on recto.

Most of these drawings were shown at the Carfax Gallery, London, April 1907; see *Catalogue of Caricatures by Max Beerbohm.* London: Carfax & Co., 1907.

Cartoons "The Second Childhood of John Bull." London: Stephen Swift & Co. [1911].

Fifteen unnumbered cartoons, lithographed in color on rectos only; each cartoon preceded by a leaf bearing a printed caption on verso.

The cartoons were shown at the Carfax Gallery, London, December 1901; see *One Hundred Caricatures by Max Beerbohm.* London: Carfax & Co., 1901.

Fifty Caricatures. London: William Heinemann, 1913.

Forty-eight unnumbered caricatures in halftone, tipped on rectos of brown mounts with descriptive letterpress at bottom; two line drawings, printed on rectos of white leaves, with title at bottom.

Some of these drawings were shown at the Leicester Galleries, London, April-May 1911 and April-May 1913; see *Catalogue of an Exhibition of One Hundred Caricatures by Max Beerbohm.* London: The Leicester Galleries, 1911, and *Catalogue of an Exhibition of Cartoons by Max Beerbohm.* London: The Leicester Galleries, 1913.

A Survey. London: William Heinemann, 1921.

Frontispiece in color; fifty-one unnumbered caricatures in halftone, tipped on rectos of mounts of heavy tan paper; each caricature preceded by a tissue guard sheet with descriptive letterpress on verso.

All but four of these drawings were chosen from the many exhibited at the Leicester Galleries, London, May-June 1921; see *Catalogue of Another Exhibition of Caricatures by Max Beerbohm.* London: The Leicester Galleries, 1921.

Rossetti and His Circle. London: William Heinemann, 1922.

Frontispiece in color; twenty-two caricatures in color, tipped on rectos of mounts of heavy tan paper; each caricature preceded by a tissue guard sheet with arabic numeral and descriptive letterpress on verso.

Eighteen of these drawings were shown at the Leicester Galleries, London, September 1921; see *Catalogue of an Exhibition of a Series of Drawings, "Rossetti and His Friends", by Max Beerbohm.* London: The Leicester Galleries, 1921.

Things New and Old. London: William Heinemann, 1923.

Frontispiece in color; forty-nine caricatures and cartoons, printed in halftone directly on rectos of leaves; each drawing preceded by a tissue guard sheet with arabic numeral and descriptive letterpress on verso.

Many of these drawings were shown at the Leicester Galleries, London, June 1923; see *Catalogue of Another Exhibition of Caricatures by Max Beerbohm.* London: The Leicester Galleries, 1923.

Observations. London: William Heinemann, 1925.

Frontispiece in color; fifty-one caricatures and cartoons, printed in half-tone and tipped on rectos of grey mounts; each drawing preceded by a tissue guard sheet with arabic numeral and descriptive letterpress on verso.

The drawings were shown at the Leicester Galleries, London, April-May 1925; see *Catalogue of Another Exhibition of Caricatures by Max Beerbohm.* London: The Leicester Galleries, 1925.

Heroes and Heroines of Bitter Sweet [London: Messrs. Leadlay, Ltd., 1931].

Portfolio containing five unnumbered "sentimental" drawings in color of members of the cast of Noel Coward's play *Bitter Sweet* (1929), tipped on rectos; each sheet preceded by a grey-blue paper guard sheet bearing printed title on recto and with stub pasted to back of main sheet.

For full bibliographical descriptions of these editions and subsequent printings see Gallatin and Oliver, pp. 4-51 passim, and Riewald 1953, pp. 255-71.

References

ARNOLD, Matthew. *Matthew Arnold: Selected Essays,* ed. Noel Annan. London: Oxford University Press, 1964.

AUDEN, W. H. "One of the Family," *Forewords and Afterwords,* ed. Edward Mendelson. New York: Random House, 1973 [pp. 367-83]; rpt. in *The Surprise of Excellence,* ed. J. G. Riewald [pp. 159-74].

BECHHOFER ROBERTS. *Paul Verlaine.* London: Jarrolds, 1937.

BEHRMAN, S. N. *Portrait of Max: An Intimate Memoir of Sir Max Beerbohm.* New York: Random House, 1960; publ. in England under the title *Conversation with Max.* London: Hamish Hamilton, 1960.

BENNETT, Arnold. *The Journals of Arnold Bennett, 1896-1931,* ed. Newman Flower. 3 vols. London: Cassell & Co., 1932-33.

BOAS, Guy. "The Magic of Max." *Blackwood's Magazine,* 260 (November 1946), 341-50; rpt. in *The Surprise of Excellence,* ed. J. G. Riewald [pp. 6-20].

BUCKLEY, Anthony John. "The Dramatic Criticism of Max Beerbohm." Diss. Cornell 1967.

BURNS, Robert. *The Poetical Works of Robert Burns,* ed. J. Logie Robertson. London: Oxford University Press, 1904.

Caricatures by Max: From the Collection in the Ashmolean Museum, ed. K. T. P. London: Oxford University Press, 1958.

CARROLL, Lewis. *The Complete Works of Lewis Carroll,* introd. Alexander Woollcott, illus. John Tenniel. London: The Nonesuch Press, n. d.

CECIL, David. *Max: A Biography*. London: Constable, 1964.

COLERIDGE, Samuel Taylor. *Specimens of the Table Talk of the late Samuel Taylor Coleridge.* 2 vols. London: John Murray, 1835 [publ. by H. N. Coleridge].

COOK, E. T. *The Life of John Ruskin.* 2 vols. London: George Allen, 1912.

DAICHES, David. *Robert Burns.* London: Longmans, Green, 1957.

——. *A Critical History of English Literature,* vol. II. London: Secker & Warburg, 1960, and New York: Ronald Press, 1970.

DE LA MARE, Walter. *The Complete Poems of Walter de la Mare.* London: Faber & Faber, 1969.

DRINKWATER, John. *Poems 1908-1914 by John Drinkwater.* London: Sidgwick & Jackson, 1917.

DUNKEL, Wilbur Dwight. *Sir Arthur Pinero: A Critical Biography with Letters.* Chicago: University of Chicago Press, 1941.

EDEL, Leon. *Henry James: The Treacherous Years 1895-1901.* London: Rupert Hart-Davis, 1969, and Philadelphia: Lippincott, 1969.

ELIOT, T. S. *Selected Essays 1917-1932.* London: Faber & Faber, 1932.

FELSTINER, John. "Max Beerbohm and the Wings of Henry James." *The Kenyon Review,* 29 (1967), 449-71; rpt. in *The Surprise of Excellence,* ed. J. G. Riewald [pp. 192-214].

——. "Changing Faces in Max Beerbohm's Caricature." *Princeton University Library Chronicle,* 33 (Winter 1972, No. 2), 73-88.

——. *The Lies of Art: Max Beerbohm's Parody and Caricature.* New York: Alfred A. Knopf, 1972, and London: Victor Gollancz, 1973; referred to as "Felstiner 1973."

FULFORD, Roger. *Osbert Sitwell.* London: Longmans, Green, 1951.

GALLATIN, A. E., and L. M. OLIVER, comps. *A Bibliography of the Works of Max Beerbohm.* The Soho Bibliographies III. London: Rupert Hart-Davis, 1952.

GAUNT, William. *The Pre-Raphaelite Tragedy.* London: Jonathan Cape, 1942.

——. *The Aesthetic Adventure.* London: Jonathan Cape, 1945.

GOETHE, Johann Wolfgang. *Sämtliche Gedichte,* vol. II. Zürich: Artemis-Verlag [1953].

GOMBRICH, E. H., and E. KRIS. *Caricature.* The King Penguin Books. Harmondsworth: Penguin Books, 1940.

GREACEN, Robert. *The Art of Noël Coward.* Aldington, Kent: The Hand and Flower Press, 1953.

GRIEVE, A. I. *The Pre-Raphaelite Period, 1848-50: The Art of Dante Gabriel Rossetti.* Hingham, Norfolk: Real World Publications, 1973.

HARDY, Thomas. *The Collected Poems of Thomas Hardy.* London: Macmillan, 1960.

HICHENS, Robert. *Yesterday: The Autobiography of Robert Hichens.* London: Cassell & Co., 1947.

HILLIER, Bevis. *Cartoons and Caricatures.* London: Studio Vista, and New York: E. P. Dutton & Co., 1970.

HOLLOWAY, Mark. *Norman Douglas: A Biography.* London: Secker & Warburg, 1976.

HOLROYD, Michael. *Lytton Strachey: A Critical Biography.* 2 vols. London: William Heinemann, 1967-68.

HONE, Joseph M. *The Life of George Moore: With an Account of his Last Years by his Cook and Housekeeper Clara Warville.* London: Victor Gollancz, 1936.

HUNT, John Dixon. *The Pre-Raphaelite Imagination 1848-1900.* London: Routledge & Kegan Paul, 1968.

HUSS, Roy Gerard. "Max Beerbohm: Critic of the Edwardian Theatre." Diss. University of Chicago 1959.

HUXLEY, Julian, ed. *Aldous Huxley, 1894-1963: A Memorial Volume.* London: Chatto & Windus, 1965.

HYDE, H. Montgomery. *Henry James at Home.* London: Methuen & Co., 1969, and New York: Farrar, Straus and Giroux, 1969.

JOHNSTON, Robert D. *Dante Gabriel Rossetti.* New York: Twayne, 1969.

LANG, Cecil. Y., ed. *The Pre-Raphaelites and their Circle: With* The Rubáiyát of Omar Khayyám. Boston: Houghton Mifflin Co., 1968.

LEAVIS, F. R. *New Bearings in English Poetry: A Study of the Contemporary Situation.* London: Chatto & Windus, 1950 [1st ed. 1932].

LEHMANN, John. *A Nest of Tigers: Edith, Osbert and Sacheverell Sitwell in their Times.* London: Macmillan, 1968.

LESLEY, Cole. *Remembered Laughter: The Life of Noel Coward.* London: Jonathan Cape, 1976, and New York: Alfred A. Knopf, 1976.

LYNCH, Bohun. *Max Beerbohm in Perspective: With a Prefatory Letter by M. B.* London: William Heinemann, 1921.

MCELDERRY, Bruce R. "Max Beerbohm: Essayist, Caricaturist, Novelist," *On Stage and Off: Eight Essays in English Literature Presented to Dr. Emmett L. Avery,* ed. John W. Erstine, John R. Elwood, and Robert C. McLean. Pullman: Washington State University Press, 1968 [pp. 76-86]; rpt. in *The Surprise of Excellence,* ed. J. G. Riewald [pp. 215-28].

———. *Max Beerbohm.* New York: Twayne, 1972.

Max's Nineties: Drawings 1892-1899, introd. Osbert Lancaster. London: Rupert Hart-Davis, 1958.

MÉGROZ R. L. *The Three Sitwells: A Biographical and Critical Study.* London: The Richards Press, 1927.

MICHALOPOULOS, André. *Homer.* New York: Twayne [1966].

MILL, John Stuart. *The Subjection of Women.* London: Longmans, 1869.

MIX, Katherine Lyon. *Max and the Americans.* Brattleboro, Vt.: The Stephen Greene Press, 1974.

O'BRIEN, Kevin H. F. "'The House Beautiful': A Reconstruction of Oscar Wilde's American Lecture." *Victorian Studies,* 17 (1974), 395-418.

PANTER-DOWNES, Mollie. *At the Pines: Swinburne and Watts-Dunton in Putney.* London: Hamish Hamilton, 1971, and Boston: Gambit, 1971.

PATMORE, Coventry. *The Poems of Coventry Patmore,* ed. Frederick Page. London: Oxford University Press, 1949.

POLWARTH, Joan. "Uncle Robert" [i.e., Robert Bontine Cunninghame Graham], *Glasgow Illustrated,* May 1976.

POUND, Reginald. *Arnold Bennett: A Biography.* London: William Heinemann, 1952.

QUENNELL, Peter. "Pre-Raphaelite Loves and Gloomy Regrets" [review], *New York Times,* 15 December 1963.

RIEWALD, J. G. *Sir Max Beerbohm, Man and Writer: A Critical Analysis with a Brief Life and a Bibliography. With a Prefatory Letter by Sir Max Beerbohm.* The Hague: Martinus Nijhoff, 1953, and Brattleboro, Vt.: The Stephen Greene Press, 1961.

_____. "Parody as Criticism." *Neophilologus,* 50 (No. 1, January 1966), 125-48.

_____, ed. *The Surprise of Excellence: Modern Essays on Max Beerbohm.* Hamden, Conn.: Archon Books, 1974.

ROSSETTI, Christina. *The Poetical Works of Christina Georgina Rossetti,* ed. William Michael Rossetti. London: Macmillan, 1904.

_____, D. G. *Letters of Dante Gabriel Rossetti,* ed. Oswald Doughty and John Robert Wahl. 4 vols. Oxford: Clarendon Press, 1965-67.

_____, D. G. *Dante Gabriel Rossetti and Jane Morris: Their Correspondence,* ed. John Bryson and Janet Camp Troxell. London: Oxford University Press, 1976.

ROTHENSTEIN, John. "Max," *The Poets' Corner by Sir Max Beerbohm.* London: The King Penguin Books, 1943, pp. 5-13; rpt. in *The Surprise of Excellence,* ed. J. G. Riewald [pp. 1-5].

Rubáiyát of Omar Khayyám . . . Rendered into English Verse. London:

Bernard Quaritch, 1879 [the fourth edition of Edward FitzGerald's translation].

STEVENSON, David Harry. "The Critical Principles and Devices of Max Beerbohm." Diss. University of Michigan 1954.

SURTEES, Virginia. *The Paintings and Drawings of Dante Gabriel Rossetti (1828-1882): A Catalogue Raisonné.* Vol. I: Text; vol. II: Plates. Oxford: Clarendon Press, 1971.

SWINBURNE, Algernon Charles. *Poems and Ballads.* London: Camden Hotton, 1866.

THOMPSON, J. W. M. "The Voice of the Prophet," *Spectator,* 4 April 1970.

TINDALL, William York. *Forces in Modern British Literature.* New York: Vintage Books, 1956.

TOWNSEND, J. Benjamin. *John Davidson: Poet of Armageddon.* New Haven: Yale University Press, 1961.

WARNER, Oliver. *Joseph Conrad.* London: Longmans, Green & Co., 1950.

WILSON, Edmund. "An Analysis of Max Beerbohm," *Classics and Commercials: A Literary Chronicle of the Forties.* New York: Farrar, Straus, 1950 [pp. 431-41]; rpt. in *The Surprise of Excellence,* ed. J. G. Riewald [pp. 38-46].

WORDSWORTH, William. *The Poetical Works of William Wordsworth,* ed. E. de Selincourt and Helen Darbishire. 5 vols. Oxford: Clarendon Press, 1940-49.

Index of Persons Caricatured

References are to plate numbers